Cowley Publications is a ministry of the brothers of the Society of Saint John the Evangelist, a monastic order in the Episcopal Church. Our mission is to provide books and resources for those seeking spiritual and theological formation. Cowley Publications is committed to developing a new generation of writers and teachers who will encourage people to think and pray in new ways about spirituality, reconciliation, and the future.

# Centering Prayer
# and
# Inner Awakening

## Cynthia Bourgeault

## Foreword by Thomas Keating

COWLEY PUBLICATIONS

*Lanham, Chicago, New York, Toronto, and Plymouth, UK*

© 2004 Cynthia Bourgeault
All rights reserved.

Published by Cowley Publications
An imprint of Rowman & Littlefield Publishers, Inc.
A wholly owned subsidiary of The Rowman & Littlefield Publishing Group, Inc.
4501 Forbes Boulevard, Suite 200
Lanham, MD 20706

Estover Road
Plymouth PL6 7PY
United Kingdom

Distributed by National Book Network

Library of Congress Cataloging-in-Publication Data:

Bourgeault, Cynthia.
    Centering prayer and inner awakening / Cynthia Bourgeault ; foreword by
Thomas Keating.
    p. cm.
    Includes bibliographical references.
    ISBN 10: 1-56101-262-9    ISBN 13: 978-1-56101-262-6    (pbk. : alk. paper)
    1. Contemplation. I. Title.
BV5091.C7B68 2004
248.3—dc22
                            2004008477

Quotation from *Living Presence* by Kabir Edmund Helminski, copyright 1992 by
Kabir Edmund Helminski. Used by permission of Jeremy P. Tarcher, an imprint of
Penguin Group (USA) Inc.

Cover design: Gary Ragaglia

This book was printed in the United States of America on acid-free paper.

# Foreword

Cynthia Bourgeault has absorbed the principles of the Christian contemplative tradition in such a way as to make them inspiring to contemporary seekers of deep prayer and union with God. Her masterful use of words enables each person to feel personally addressed and invited by the divine Spirit into the spiritual journey, and to the practice of Centering Prayer in particular.

Her focus in this book is the contribution she perceives that Centering Prayer can make to the renewal and appropriate adaptation of the Christian contemplative heritage to the circumstances of our time. She applies her singular grasp of the Centering Prayer practice to the needs both of beginners and of those who are advancing in faith and love toward the experience of divine union to which the Gospel of Jesus Christ and the integral practice of the Christian religion relentlessly invite us.

There are a significant number of excellent distinctions and clarifications in this book. These will help those in the spiritual network hosted by Contemplative Outreach to strengthen their commitment to the practice of Centering Prayer and to deepen their understanding of its theological and spiritual roots.

Here are a few of those major points:

The distinction between cataphatic and apophatic contemplation (Chapter 5), and particularly the description of the difficulties that may ensue when one attempts to practice apophatic prayer with a cataphatic mindset.

*Lectio divina* (Chapter 6) as a necessary companion, along with appropriate communal prayer and rituals, to the inner solitude and silence cultivated in Centering Prayer.

The kenotic character of Centering Prayer (Chapter 8) that participates in the primordial movement of love within the Trinity, expressed through the emptying of the Father into the Son and the emptying of the Son into all creation through the incarnation.

Attention of the heart (Chapters 9 and 11), where the author distinguishes between the basic receptivity of Centering Prayer and the concentrative character of mindfulness practices in other spiritual traditions, both Eastern and Western. The clarity of mind that the latter normally seek is an excellent preparation for contemplative prayer (or meditation in the terms of the Eastern religions). Centering Prayer, inspired by the tradition of the Desert Fathers and Mothers, emphasizes purity of heart, which is a disposition of humility and pure love leading to total self-surrender. Indeed, to distinguish Centering Prayer from practices of concentrative attention, we might call it "heartfulness" practice. I especially appreciated the introduction of an element of Eastern Orthodox spirituality that throws powerful light on the issue.

The inner observer (Chapter 12) as a bridge from interior silence to the blooming of the True Self in which the unity and diversity of God and each person of the Trinity can be lived and manifested in daily life and in all circumstances.

The Welcoming Prayer (Chapter 13) as a practical way of self-surrender in daily life and in the present moment and which complements the passive letting go of all perceptions in Centering Prayer, leading to interior silence and to the prayer in secret so highly recommended by Jesus himself (Matthew 6:6).

Cynthia's outstanding treatment of the subtleties of Centering Prayer invites the reflection of qualified practitioners and meditators. These are areas that need to be illumined by the experience and insight of long-term practitioners as Contemplative Outreach reaches its twentieth birthday and knocks on the doors of seminaries and postgraduate institutions of all kinds.

The work that I have done has been addressed primarily to beginners seeking a serious Christian practice which is not only oriented to the grace of divine union but can also provide inspiration and support for the demanding ministries of service that are multiplying in our time. Centering Prayer is aimed at healing the violence in ourselves and purifying the unconscious of its hidden and flawed motivation that reduces and can even cancel out the effectiveness of the external works of mercy, justice, and peace.

My special and heartfelt thanks to Cynthia for her monumental contribution to the better understanding of the Centering Prayer practice and its immediate conceptual background, thus making it more accessible to the ever-growing number of seekers of our time.

Thomas Keating

# Acknowledgments and Dedication

This book is the product of many hearts and minds and would never have come into being apart from that collaboration. My thanks go first and foremost to Margaret Haines and Sandy Gordon, founding matriarch and patriarch of The Contemplative Society in Victoria, British Columbia, whose strength, wisdom, and Scottish tenacity have sustained me through thick and thin as together we birthed a new organization and grew deeper in our understanding and practice of the Centering Prayer.

To Heather Page, administrative assistant of the Contemplative Society, who has been my right-hand person at every step of the way, and whose gracious presence and impeccable organizational skills have so supported the flourishing of Centering Prayer in this corner of Canada.

To the many laborers in the vineyard who have taught workshops, facilitated groups, or supported retreats from the "command post" in the kitchen: especially Anita Boyd, Christopher Page, Brian Mitchell, Flo Masson, Bronwen Boddington, Glenna Tiedje, Katherine Jarrett, and Suzanne Manley; and to the many,

many others who have attended these events over the years and through their keen presence and deep, questing spirits have encouraged my own emerging voice as a teacher and writer.

To Leslie Canil, who patiently hand-transcribed hours of taped workshops to create the core manuscript for this book; to Barbara Huston, coordinator emeritus of Contemplative Outreach Northwest in Seattle, whose irrepressible enthusiasm for working collaboratively opened doors both internationally and interspiritually; and to Anne Henderson, current president of the Contemplative Society, whose vision and faith pulled us through a difficult transitional year.

To Father Tom Francis, ocso, of the Monastery of the Holy Spirit in Conyers, Georgia, who read an early draft of the manuscript and offered his encouragement and deep insights on the apophatic life; and to Joan Maxwell, whose staunch support both emotionally and financially made the crucial difference in this book actually seeing the light of day.

To the Contemplative Outreach National staff, especially Gail Fitzpatrick-Hopler, who have been wonderfully receptive to my manuscript and have contributed many helpful suggestions and updated materials; and to Michael Wilt, my editor at Cowley Publications, who guided this project through the editing and production phases with a deft hand and admirable equanimity.

And above all to Thomas Keating, my friend, mentor, and teacher, to whom this book is gratefully dedicated. Aside from providing the original inspiration and *raison d'être* for this book, Father Thomas was also strongly present for me at the finish line as I polished off the writing during a whirlwind Christmas retreat "on location" in Colorado. For nearly three weeks he gave unstintingly of his time, poring over each chapter (including catching typos and spelling errors), engaging in patient dialogue about those places where we saw things differently, and in all ways honoring this project with his enthusiasm and wisdom. For me, this is the real blessing and transmission conveyed in this book, of which my words are merely the grateful recipients.

# Introduction

"**W**hy do we need yet another book on Centering Prayer?" a friend of mine asked when I told her the topic of my new manuscript.

"Oh, I see why," she said when she had finished reading it. I hope that will be your response as well.

It's true that Centering Prayer is a highly visible topic these days. Its principal architect and spokesperson, Father Thomas Keating, has graced the front cover of *Common Boundary* and a number of other spiritual magazines, and his public appearances draw packed audiences. Contemplative Outreach, the organization he founded in 1984, has a mailing list of some 100,000 people worldwide. Within and beyond this network, publishers are kept busy packaging and repackaging his books, videos, and audio tapes along with those of an emerging crop of protégées.

But although there is tremendous enthusiasm within the movement itself, and in its spillover into New Age and wellness movements, what has long concerned me is the lack of real ownership for this practice within the classic institutions of Christian nurture: churches, seminaries and schools of theology, and main-stream theological scholarship and publication. Much of the excitement is really "preaching to the choir." There is still relatively little formation in this practice among church leaders, and little critical feedback. While much admired, Thomas Keating is rarely challenged openly or drawn into dialogue on the more subtle points of his innovative teaching. There is still little real understanding of how Centering Prayer is related to the classic tradition of Christian contemplation, and virtually no appreciation of the distinct nuances of its methods or of its revolutionary (and still largely untapped) potential to transform Christian life.

*Centering Prayer and Inner Awakening* is intended as a complete guidebook for all who wish to know the practice better. I hope this book will encourage and extend the dialogue of which I have just spoken. But more important, I hope it will get you up and running in the practice itself; or, if you are already practicing, that it will widen your understanding of the prayer's theological and spiritual context and provide additional food for your own journey.

I have been a practitioner of Centering Prayer since 1988, and I can gratefully say that it has changed my life and the way I understand Christianity. When I first encountered the practice I had been an Episcopal priest for nearly a decade, a great lover of the Christian mystical and inner traditions, and a veteran retreat-goer. But I had never had any luck establishing a meditation practice. I hated to admit it, but the process of trying to nail down and tether my mind, to focus it on a mantra— even the Jesus Prayer— brought howls of inner resistance. I had pretty much given up when I encountered Centering Prayer, and through its uniquely forgiving starting point found my way into meditation at last. The practice took, and I have been with it ever since.

I received the training and commissioning as a presenter of Centering Prayer, served on the National Faculty of Contemplative Outreach from 1990 to 1995, and had the honor of working closely with Thomas Keating as the editor of two of his books, *Invitation to Love* and *Intimacy with God*. He continues to be my teacher and mentor, and I am profoundly in his debt, not only for what he has taught me, but for the opportunities and challenges he has opened up for me and his steadfast support during those times of transition and "spiritual combat."

But it's also true that I came to Centering Prayer with somewhat different reference points from Keating himself and many others in the network, primarily because of my background in the Christian inner tradition. In my earlier years of spiritual seeking I had encountered the Gurdjieff Work, a comprehensive system of inner awakening with deep roots in the ancient Wisdom traditions of Central Asia and the Christian Near East. Through nearly ten years of participation in "the Work" I was familiar with the classic building blocks of inner transformation: attention, conscious presence, and the development of a strong inner observer (or witnessing presence); and it was through this training that I began to glimpse the deeper potential of Centering Prayer in the service of inner awakening; or in other words, as an authentic Wisdom path.

In 1997, after six years in full- or part-time residence near Thomas Keating at St. Benedict's Monastery in Snowmass, Colorado, I was invited by a group of contemplatives in British Columbia to move north and help them found a network to support contemplative growth in that part of the world. The Contemplative Society came into being in 1997, centered in the city of Victoria. One of the fortuitous aspects of its birth was that its founders were, in about equal numbers, practitioners not only of Centering Prayer but also of Christian Meditation, a parallel method developed by the Benedictine abbot John Main. From the start, then, the Contemplative Society was a bit independent of the more formalized teaching curriculum of Contemplative Outreach and had to make its way in dialogue with another meditation tradition. A good opportunity for growth! Thomas Keating graciously encouraged this experimentation and gave us the space to develop alternative teaching strategies and presentational formats appropriate to our own circumstances.

What you'll find in this book is the fruit of this experimentation: Centering Prayer as it's been lived, worked through, and discussed among people in British Columbia and in close association with Contemplative Outreach groups in the Pacific Northwest.

As I said earlier, my focus here is first and foremost practical: to get you up and running in the practice. You'll see that Part I walks you through the steps, starting at the very beginning— no previous experience necessary! The second and third parts situate Centering Prayer within the Christian contemplative tradition, and to comment from this perspective on both its traditional and innovative aspects.

Part IV widens the scope considerably, both theoretically and practically, as I attempt to build a bridge between Centering Prayer and the traditional language and methodology of inner awakening. Some of the material here is quite new and has never appeared in print anywhere before. In venturing to break this new ground, my guiding understanding has been that inner work is a way of accepting the profound invitation (in Philippians 2:5) to "have in yourselves the same mind as Christ."

Whoever you are, or whatever your spiritual reference points, I hope you'll feel invited into this book: clergy, theologians, and spiritual directors trying to understand why Centering Prayer actually belongs in the Christian tradition; meditators trying to understand the distinct nuances of the method; ordinary Christians trying to find a practice that actually transforms their lives. Whatever your starting points may be, my sense is both that this work is important and that it's important for us to undertake it together. At a time in our Christian life when the factional extremes, like the proverbial two cats of Kilkenny, seem intent on fighting each other to death while the rest of the world goes its way in massive indifference, I know from my own experience that there is something in this prayer that can restore harmony, dignity, and depth to our lived Christian community. It is this, more than anything else that I wish to share with you.

# PART I

## The Method of Centering Prayer

# 1 ⑥ Contemplative Prayer and Centering Prayer

*Prayer is not a request for God's favors. True, it has been used to obtain the satisfaction of personal desires. It has even been adopted to reinforce prejudices, justify violence, and create barriers between people and between countries. But genuine prayer is based on recognizing the Origin of all that exists, and opening ourselves to it. . . . In prayer we acknowledge God as the supreme source from which flows all strength, all goodness, all existence, acknowledging that we have our being, life itself from this supreme Power. One can then communicate with this Source, worship it, and ultimately place one's very center in it.*

Piero Ferrucci, *Ineffable Grace* (p. 254)

"**P**rayer is talking to God": with these words nearly all of us receive our first religious instruction. Certainly I did. As a child, I learned the usual first prayers and graces ("Now I lay me down to sleep" and "God is great, God is good . . ."), followed, a bit later, by the Lord's Prayer and the Twenty-Third Psalm. I was also encouraged to speak to God in my own words and instructed that the appropriate topics for this conversation were to give thanks for the blessings of the day and to ask for assistance with particular needs and concerns.

But for all this, I was also one of the relatively rare few who also had it patterned into me that prayer was *listening* to God. Not even listening for messages, exactly, like the child Samuel in my favorite Old Testament story, but just being there, quietly gathered in God's presence. This learning came not from my formal Sunday School training, but through the good fortune of spending my first six school years in a Quaker school, where weekly silent "meeting for worship" was as an invariable part of the rhythm of life as schoolwork or recess. I can still remember trooping together, class by class, into the cavernous two-story meetinghouse and taking our places on the long, narrow benches once occupied by elders of yore. Occasionally, there would be a scriptural verse or thought offered, but for long stretches there was simply silence. And in that silence, as I gazed up at the sunlight sparkling through those high upper windows, or followed a secret tug drawing me

4

down into my own heart, I began to know a prayer much deeper than "talking to God." Somewhere in those depths of silence I came upon my first experiences of God as a loving presence that was always near, and prayer as a simple trust in that presence.

Almost four decades later, when I was introduced to Centering Prayer through the work of Father Thomas Keating, it did not take me long to recognize where I was. In a deep way I'd come home again to that place I first knew as a child in Quaker meeting.

What I know now, of course, is that the type of prayer I was being exposed to during those meetings for worship was contemplative prayer. In Christian spiritual literature, this term all too often has the aura of being an advanced and somewhat rarified form of prayer, mostly practiced by monks and mystics. But in essence, contemplative prayer is simply a wordless, trusting opening of self to the divine presence. Far from being advanced, it is about the simplest form of prayer there is. Children recognize it instantly—as I did—perhaps because, as the sixteenth-century mystic John of the Cross intimates, "Silence is God's first language."[1] At our Quaker school no one ever made a big deal of it. In fact, we never received any instruction on how to do it at all, because it was sensed among the Quakers to be so supremely *natural*, like a baby duck taking to water.

As we grow up, of course, our minds grow more complex and more settled in their own orbits. We spend so much of our adult energies thinking, planning, worrying, trying to get ahead or stay afloat, that we lose touch with that natural intimacy with God deep within us. The gift of silence gradually recedes in the face of the demands of daily life, so that when we do re-encounter contemplative prayer as adults, it may seem like a strange and inaccessible inner terrain. With some effort, we can stop the outer noise. Silent walks in the woods, Lenten and Advent quiet days at the local church, or a retreat at a monastery are wonderful ways of doing just that. But stopping the inner noise is another matter. Even when the outer world has been wrestled into silence, we still go right on talking, worrying, arguing with ourselves, daydreaming, fantasizing. To encounter those deeper reaches of our being, where our own life is constantly flowing out of and back into the divine life, what first seems to be needed is some sort of an interior on/off switch to tone down the inner talking as well.

That's probably the simplest way to picture what Centering Prayer is, and to describe its relationship to contemplative prayer. At root, it is a very simple method for reconnecting us with that natural aptitude for the inner life, that simplicity of our childhood, once our adult minds have become overly complex and busy.

It's very, very simple. You sit, either in a chair or on a prayer stool or mat, and allow your heart to open toward that invisible but always present Origin of all that exists. Whenever a thought comes into your mind, you simply let the thought go and return to that open, silent attending upon the depths. Not because thinking is bad, but because it pulls you back to the surface of yourself. You use a short word or phrase, known as a "sacred word," such as "abba" (Jesus' own word for God) or "peace" or "be still" to help you let go of the thought promptly and cleanly. You do this practice for twenty minutes, a bit longer if you'd like, then you simply get up and move on with your life.

What goes on in those silent depths during the time of Centering Prayer is no one's business, not even your own; it is between your innermost being and God; that place where, as St. Augustine once said, "God is closer to your soul than you are yourself." Your own subjective experience of the prayer may be that nothing happened—except for the more-or-less continuous motion of letting go of thoughts. But in the depths of your being, in fact, plenty has been going on, and things are quietly but firmly being rearranged. That interior rearrangement—or to give it its rightful name, that interior *awakening*—is the real business of Centering Prayer, and of this book.

# 2 ⑥ Deeper Silence, Deeper Self

"**S**ilence is God's first language," says the sixteenth-century mystic John of the Cross. And silence is the normal context in which contemplative prayer takes place. But as we saw in the last chapter, there is silence and then there is silence. There is an outer silence, an outer stopping of the words and busy-ness, but there is also a much more challenging interior silence, where the inner talking stops as well.

Most of us are familiar with this first kind of silence, although we don't get enough of it in our spiritual nurture. It's the kind of silence we normally practice in retreat times and quiet days; sometimes you'll hear it described as "free silence." With a break from the usual hurly-burly of your life, you have time to draw inward and allow your mind to meander. You may pore over a scriptural verse and let your imagination and feelings carry you more deeply into it. Or you may simply put the books away and go for a walk in the woods, allowing the tranquility of the setting and the relative quieting of external pressures to bring you more deeply in touch with yourself. You listen carefully to how you're

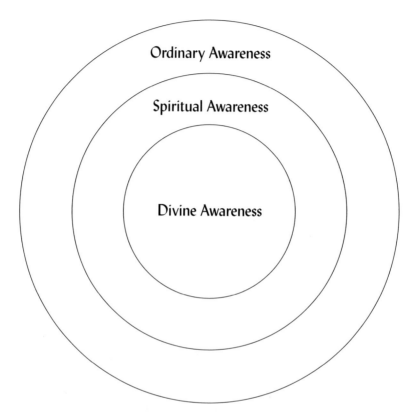

feeling, what you're wishing. In this kind of work, the free association of your mind provides the key to the renewal, and silence furnishes the backdrop where this work can go on.

But there is another kind of silence as well, far less familiar to most Christians. In this other kind of silence, the drill is exactly the opposite. In free silence, you encourage your mind to float where it will; in this other, sometimes called "intentional silence"—or to use the generic description, *meditation*—a deliberate effort is made to restrain the wandering of the mind, either by slowing down the thought process itself or by developing a means of detaching oneself from it.

Intentional silence almost always feels like work. It doesn't come naturally to most people, and there is in fact considerable resistance raised from the mind itself: "You mean I just *sit* there and make my mind a blank?" Then the inner talking begins in earnest, and you ask yourself, "How can this be prayer? How can God give me my imagination, reason, and feelings and then expect me not to use them?" "Where do 'I' go to if I stop thinking?" "Is it safe?"

Since Centering Prayer is a discipline of intentional silence, dealing with this internal resistance is an inevitable part of developing a practice. In fact, I've often said to participants at Centering Prayer introductory workshops that ninety percent of the trick in successfully establishing a practice lies in wanting to do it in the first place. So let's consider that question first.

## The Art of Awakening

Perhaps the most powerful argument is the one from authority. Virtually every spiritual tradition that holds a vision of human transformation at its heart also claims that a practice of intentional silence is a non-negotiable. Period. You just have to do it. Whether it be the meditation of the yogic and Buddhist traditions, the *zikr* of the Sufis, the *devkut* of mystical Judaism, or the contemplative prayer of the Christians, there is a universal affirmation that this form of spiritual practice is essential to spiritual awakening.

When I talk about "transformation" and "awakening," incidentally, I should make clear that I am not using New Age terminology. I am speaking of: "You must be born from above" (John 3:7 NRSV), or "Unless a grain of wheat fall into the earth and dies, it remains just a single grain; but if it dies, it bears much fruit" (John 12:24), or perhaps most pointedly: "For whoever wants to save his life will lose it, and whoever loses his life for me will find it" (Matthew 16:24–25). Among the worldwide religions, Christianity is surely one of those most urgently and irrevocably set upon the total transformation of the human person. And while it's true that we don't have pictures of Jesus teaching meditation practice exactly—this can be read between the lines fairly easily on any number of occasions[1] and more important, derived theologically, which will be the subject of Chapter 8.

9

Like most the great spiritual masters of our universe, Jesus taught from the conviction that we human beings are victims of a tragic case of mistaken identity. The person I normally take myself to be—that busy, anxious little "I" so preoccupied with its goals, fears, desires, and issues—is never even remotely the whole of who I am, and to seek the fulfillment of my life at this level means to miss out on the bigger life. This is why, according to his teaching, the one who tries to keep his "life" (i.e., the small one) will lose it, and the one who is willing to lose it will find the real thing. Beneath the surface there is a deeper and vastly more authentic Self, but its presence is usually veiled by the clamor of the smaller "I" with its insatiable needs and demands.

This confusion between small self and larger Self (variously known in the traditions as "True Self," "Essential Self," or "Real I") is the core illusion of the human condition, and penetrating this illusion is what awakening is all about.

## Beyond Ordinary Awareness

But why is intentional silence so important to this process of awakening? One of the most effective ways of getting at this question comes through a simple bull's-eye diagram created by Father Thomas Keating. It's called "Levels of Awareness."

The outer circle is called our "Ordinary Awareness." This is the mind as it usually thinks, and our sense of self tied to that way of thinking.

As human beings we are gifted with what is known as "self-reflexive consciousness": the capacity to stand outside ourselves and look upon ourselves in the third person. Because of this unique capacity of the mind (as far as we know, we're the only species so gifted), we are able to experience ourselves as unique persons, made up of unique qualities, capacities, and needs. The subject/object polarity built into the way the mind works sets up the impression of "having" a distinct identity, informed by certain attributes and imbued with certain gifts that need to become fully expressed if my personhood is to be whole. That sets up a good

10

deal of expectation—and also a good deal of anxiety.

If one really follows closely what thinking and selfhood feel like at this ordinary level, it is not a pretty picture. Into our head, out of nowhere, pop random thoughts, memories, associations, and sensations. Sometimes they are stimulated by the environment; more often by the environment triggering a memory or triggering a reaction or chain reaction.

I remember testing this for myself once. I had read somewhere that without spiritual training the human mind is unable to concentrate on anything for more than two minutes. Surely this must be wrong, I thought; with a Ph.D. and a couple of books under my belt, I figured my powers of concentration must be considerably better than that. So to test this theory, I set myself the task of noticing everything red in the next five-mile stretch of highway I was driving.

What a humiliation! I did all right for the first thirty seconds or so, until the next red thing that popped into my path happened to be a Dairy Queen. When I "woke up" again, several miles later, I realized I had been completely lost in a long reverie touched off by childhood memories of ice cream at the beach. So much for my superior powers of concentration!

The Buddhists smilingly call this "monkey mind." The little beast jumps from one tree limb to the other, taking the whole of us with it. And we would probably not be able to abide the inner chaos were it not for that stable sense of "self" created through the subject/object polarity. At the center of all that orbiting chaos, an apparent solidity is given by that self-reflexive "I," with its constant set of self-referential questions with which it probes and measures the universe: "How well am I doing?" "Is it safe here?" "What did she mean by that?" "Am I okay?"

Another name for "ordinary awareness" is "egoic thinking." It is the normal functioning zone of the human mind. It doesn't matter whether you're a Ph.D., a bishop, a nuclear physicist; how brilliantly intellectual or intensely devout you may be. Without special spiritual training, your sense of the world and your sense of yourself will be formed at this level of awareness. Even the so-called self-awareness tools of our times, from psychotherapy to Myers-Briggs personality typing to the enneagram, spend most of their effort merely resorting and clarifying the characteristics: "I am an INFP," "a gut-centered type," "a five," etc. This may yield insights into the workings of the personality, but it's still ordinary awareness.

Deeper than this, in every single one of us though unbeknownst to most of us, is the level that Thomas Keating describes as our "spiritual awareness." "Awareness" might be too mental a word to describe it, however; the sensation is much more visceral, more like that tug I experienced as a child in Quaker meeting, drawing me down into my depths. You might picture it as a kind of interior compass whose magnetic north is always fixed on God. It's there; it's as much a part of what holds you in life as your breathing or your heartbeat. And its purpose, just like a compass, is for orientation.

The problem is that most of us are not in touch with our spiritual awareness (or at least, not deeply and consistently enough in touch with it), let alone having any idea of what it's there for or how to use it. It comes upon us only rarely, sometimes in a moment of overpowering emotion, such as suddenly being moved to tears by watching a sunset or receiving the Eucharist. That "nostalgia for the divine" sweeps over us and we are left trembling before the presence of a Mystery almost more vivid and beautiful than we can bear. But ordinary life does not encourage such moments, and the impression fades, to be revisited only in our dreams, the usual repository of our spiritual awareness.

But spiritual awareness is actually a way of perceiving, just as ordinary awareness is a way of perceiving. And as with ordinary awareness, there is a sense of identity or selfhood generated through this mode of perception. The big difference between them is that whereas ordinary awareness perceives through self-reflexive consciousness, which splits the world into subject and object;

spiritual awareness perceives through an intuitive grasp of the whole and an innate sense of belonging. It's something like sounding the note G on the piano and instantly hearing the D and the B that surround it and make it a chord. And since spiritual awareness is perception based on harmony, the sense of selfhood arising out of it is not plagued by that sense of isolation and anxiety that dominates life at the ordinary level of awareness.

## The Divine Indwelling

If we have within us a compass pointing to the magnetic north of God, does this mean that God dwells within us, as the center of our being? Is that what the bull's-eye of Thomas Keating's diagram is all about—what he calls our "divine awareness"?

Cautiously, the answer to this question is "yes." I say "cautiously" because Christian theology makes very clear that the human being is not God and that the innermost core of our being is not itself divine. And yet theology has always upheld the reality of the "divine indwelling." As we move toward center, our own being and the divine being become more and more mysteriously interwoven. "There is in the soul a something in which God dwells, and there is in the soul a something in which the soul dwells in God," writes the medieval mystic Meister Eckhart, the subtlety of his words reflecting the delicacy of the motion.[2] In our own times, Thomas Merton describes this "something" in a passage of astonishing clarity and beauty:

> At the center of our being is a point of nothingness which is untouched by sin and illusion, a point of pure truth, a point or spark which belongs entirely to God, which is never at our disposal, from which God disposes of our lives, which is inaccessible to the fantasies of our own mind or the brutalities of our own will. This little point of nothingness and of absolute poverty is the pure glory of God written in us, as our poverty, as our indigence, as our sonship. It is like a pure diamond blazing with the invisible light of heaven. It is in everybody, and if we could see it, we would see these billions of points of light coming together in the face and blaze of a sun that would make all the dark-

13

ness and cruelty of life vanish completely. I have no program for this seeing. It is only given. But the gate of heaven
is everywhere.[3]

Notice how deftly Merton navigates the tricky theological
waters here. His words are bold, in that he claims—to my knowledge more clearly than any other Christian mystical writer—that
at the center of our being is an innermost point of truth which
shares not only the likeness, but perhaps even the *substance* of
God's own being. And yet, following the bent of Christian tradition, he makes it absolutely clear that access to this center is not
at our command; it is entered only through the gateway of our
complete poverty and nothingness.

The divine indwelling is the cornerstone of contemplative
prayer. Thomas Keating refers to it as "our personal big bang," for
it reveals the Source of our own being—the explosion of divine
love into form which first gave rise to our personal life. It also reveals the direction in which our hearts must travel for a constantly
renewed intimacy with this Source. As we enter contemplative
prayer, we draw near the wellspring from which our being flows.

## Mary and Martha

Another way of picturing this teaching on "levels of awareness"
is to think of it in terms of the gospel story of Mary and Martha
(Luke 10:38–41). This allows us to put a human face to each of
these three levels of awareness and to observe some of the implications for our human interactions.

Jesus has been invited to dinner; and Martha, whom we'll
say is the embodiment of ordinary awareness, is doing all the
things that are characteristic of ordinary awareness. She's busy,
she's efficient, she's getting the necessary tasks accomplished.
She's also, you may notice, stressed out, judgmental, self-righteousness, and not above manipulation if it suits her needs: "Lord,
don't you care that my sister has left me to do all the work by
myself? Please tell her to help me." You hear that self-pitying, self-
meritorious voice so typical of ordinary awareness: "I'm doing

something important and I want everybody to appreciate me."

By contrast, we have spiritual awareness as embodied by Mary, who is simply sitting in complete, rapt attunement to the divine, indwelling presence: Jesus. The two of them, Mary and Jesus together, make a perfect picture of how spiritual awareness attends to the divine awareness. She's at the feet of her lord; she's in worship. For Mary, preparing dinner is not an issue; she's already at the banquet table.

It's not that Martha is "wrong" and Mary is "right." Both types of awareness are necessary for functioning in this world. But the idea in spiritual transformation is to integrate and reprioritize these levels so that our ordinary awareness is in alignment with and in service to our spiritual awareness (which in turn, as we have seen, is in service to the divine awareness). In that alignment our being flows rightly, from innermost out. When something needs to be done in the outer world, we have sufficient ego strength to do it. But unlike ordinary awareness, which is always doing things to assert itself or fulfill itself, action grounded in our spiritual awareness merely flows out the divine abundance without regard to outcome or any need to draw attention to itself.

If we could picture our plight, then, in this usual state of our being, which spiritual masters from time immemorial have described as "sleep," we could say that each one of us has a Mary deep within us, glued to the feet of the Master. There are incredible luminous depths within in which we know how to listen and to whom we are listening. But the clarity of our listening is obscured because out on the periphery we also have a Martha who thinks that the whole world is riding on her back and drowns out the inner music with her constant barrage of "I need," "I want," "Pay attention to me."

## Putting a Stick in the Spoke of Thinking
It is right here that intentional silence enters the picture.

Our ordinary awareness, as we have seen, rests on the self-reflexive capacity of the human mind. It derives from that peculiarly human capacity to split the field of vision into subject and object and perceive oneself in the third person. If you like computer metaphors, you might say that your ordinary sense of selfhood is a function of the operating system you're using. The more you think from ordinary awareness, the more you experience yourself as separate egoic identity, defined by the particular set of characteristics, aptitudes, needs, and desires that go to make up *you*. Ordinary thinking and egoic identity go hand in hand; in fact, the two go round and round like cogwheels, in a completely closed circuit.

If you wish to experience what lies beneath, spiritual tradition teaches, the first step is simply to pull the plug on that constant self-reflexive activity of the mind. And that's what intentional silence, or meditation, is set up to do. It's like putting a stick in the spoke of thinking, so that the whole closed circuit gets derailed and the more subtle awareness at the depths of your being can begin to make its presence known.

This is not how it feels to your egoic identity, of course. From the point of view of ordinary awareness, intentional silence feels like a vacuum. That's where all the "You mean I just sit there and make my mind a blank?" complaining comes from. But it's not really a vacuum down there, and even though some of the favorite spiritual metaphors for this state have to do with "the dark night" or "cloud of unknowing," this is only true in comparison to the usual glaring neon light of our ordinary awareness. In fact, you could say that learning to shift to seeing with your spiritual awareness is a lot like learning to see in the dark. At first everything seems totally black. But if you're patient and don't grab for the flashlight, little by little you begin to discover that you can pick out shadows and shapes, and in some mysterious way "see."

And so meditation rests on the wager that if you can simply break the tyranny of your ordinary awareness, the rest will begin to unfold itself.

At first when you begin a practice of meditation, it feels like a place you go to. You may think of it as "my inner sanctuary" or "my place apart with God." But as the practice becomes more and more established in you so that this inner sanctuary begins to flow out into your life, it becomes more and more a place you come from. It is a bedrock of spiritual intelligence, a sense of connectedness known from so deeply within you that nothing can shake it. This is the ground of what tradition calls theological hope, "the hope that can never be taken away," because you simply *know* your abiding union in this place of interconnection; you know that nothing can possibly fall out of God, and that, as St. Paul so profoundly expressed it, "Whether I live or die, I am the Lord's." This is really not a statement that can be made from the level of ordinary awareness; ordinary awareness is just too frightened! Because it perceives itself as separate, it will always perceive itself as at least somewhat endangered. Only from the level of spiritual awareness do you begin to see and trust that all is held in the divine Mercy. But once grounded in that certainty, you can begin to reach out to the world with the same wonderful, generous vulnerability that we see in Christ.

"Perfect love casts out fear" (1 John 4:18). This is the core of Christ's own most authentic self-understanding, and it is the source of our own authenticity and power as Christians as well. But in my own efforts to live the gospel I have found that it is virtually impossible to reach and sustain that level of "perfect love" without a practice of contemplative prayer because the spiritual awareness must be deeply engaged before the underlying abundance is seen. Ordinary awareness always eventually betrays itself and returns to its usual postures of self-defense and self-justification.

You sometimes hear that this kind of prayer is private or narcissistic, and from the outside it may look that way: each person sitting on his or her meditation stool, wrapped up in his or her personal silence. Later in this book we may see how what goes on at the energetic level during this prayer is neither private nor without its profound effects in the physical world, a secret that hermits and mystics have always known. For now, however, as we begin to set ourselves to learning the discipline of Centering Prayer, I'd like to think that we do so in service of the gospel, to increase our capacity to become followers of Christ. The intent is not to escape into some private holiness trip, but to allow the gospel to become more and more alive in us, more and more firmly rooted. Till at last, in the words of that remarkable prayer in Ephesians 3:16–19 (NIV), which is really the charter of contemplative prayer:

> I pray that out of his glorious riches He may strengthen you with power through his Spirit in your inner being so that Christ may dwell in your hearts through faith. And I pray that you, being rooted and grounded in love, may have power, together with all the saints, to grasp how wide and long and high and deep is the love of Christ, and to know this love that surpasses knowledge—that you may be filled with the very nature of God.

# 3 ⑥ The Method of Centering Prayer

As I remarked in the last chapter, ninety percent of the battle in establishing a regular discipline of meditation lies in wanting to do it in the first place. This chapter deals with the final ten percent.

Meditation, we've seen, is essentially about putting a stick into the spokes of our normal whirling wheel of thinking in order to break up the tyranny of the mind and the sense of selfhood that goes with it. Thomas Keating rather humorously describes the process as "taking a brief vacation from yourself." All meditation practices share this basic aim. But while their purpose remains similar, the strategies for achieving it vary considerably from method to method. Centering Prayer has a very distinct angle of approach, with some striking particularities that set it off from most other methods, no matter how superficially similar. It's helpful to be aware of these particularities in advance, in order to side-step some of the usual difficult spots in the practice and to avail oneself fully of its remarkable transformative effects.

## Attention and Intention

Generally speaking, the various methodologies of meditation can be divided into three main groups: concentrative methods, awareness methods, and surrender methods. Centering prayer belongs to this last (and least common) category.

Concentrative methods, which are probably the most universal and time-honored, rely on the principle of attention. In this type of meditation, the mind is given a simple task to focus its attention on—or more accurately, *in*. Depending on the tradition, this might involve counting one's breaths, bringing attention to and then holding it on a particular area of the body (such as an arm or a leg); or, most commonly, reciting a mantra either aloud or silently.

A *mantra* is a word or short phrase of sacred origin and intent, used to collect the mind and invoke the divine presence. Some classic mantras, of course, include the great "Om padme" and "Gate, gate para gate" of the Eastern traditions, and the "La ilaha ill Allahu" ("there is nothing but God") of Islamic tradition. But prayer with a mantra is also well attested in Christian tradition, including the Jesus prayer of the Christian Orthodox, the rosary, and the *"Maranatha"*—"Come, Lord"—recommended by John Main as the foundational mantra of Christian Meditation. Some traditions (such as those reflected in Transcendental Meditation) consider the vibration of the mantra to be as important as its content, and a mantra will be specifically assigned by the teacher in order to resonate with certain aspects of the student's inner being. This aspect seems to be far less emphasized in Christian teaching.[1]

Whatever the method, the mantra provides a touchstone for the attention. Rather than allowing the mind to wander, it is anchored steadily and constantly in the simple repetition of the task. The mind stays alert and present while the deeper waters of one's being are refreshed in the numinous presence which the mantra itself invokes.

Awareness methods are much favored in Buddhist practice, particularly in Vipassana, or Insight Meditation. In awareness meditation, one aligns oneself with an inner observer and simply

20

watches the play of energy as thoughts and emotions rise, take form, and dissipate. If an angry thought emerges, rather than getting tangled up in it one simply watches—or perhaps labels it, "thinking, thinking" or "angry thinking, angry thinking." In awareness practice one learns to separate radically from one's psychological being (or ordinary awareness) and to sink deep roots into the field of consciousness itself. The fruits of this type of meditation tend to be a laser-like clarity and a fierce, unshakable *presence.*

A surrender method is even simpler. One does not even watch or label the thought as it comes up, takes form, and dissipates. As soon as it emerges into consciousness, one simply lets it go. The power of this form of meditation does not reside in a particular clarity of the mind or even in presence, but entirely in the gesture of release itself. Thomas Keating likes to characterize it as a prayer "not of attention, but of intention."

Of course, even in the more concentrative practices, intention underlies attention. One does not stay present to one's mantra without a strong intention to do so. But what's different in Centering Prayer is that it bypasses focused attention and works directly with intention itself—or with what the fourteenth-century spiritual classic *The Cloud of Unknowing* (Centering Prayer's primary source) calls our "naked intent direct to God."[2] Because there is no specific focus for the attention and no demand for a strong "I am here" presence, the prayer has a certain fluid or even dreamy quality to it that can be initially disconcerting to those accustomed to more rigorous attention-based methods. Later in this book we'll discover some of the advantages of working with this more relaxed attention, but for now it's important to realize that if you are coming to Centering Prayer from a concentrative or awareness practice, the first step may be to unlearn most of what you know. Surrender meditation has its own distinct way of getting there.

## "A naked intent direct to God . . ."

In Centering Prayer, then, everything begins in and keeps coming back to intention. What am I really up to in this prayer? What is my aim as I sit down on my chair or prayer stool and set this practice in motion?

Of course, it's difficult to put words around an experience that is deeply personal and intuitive. But in general, you're in the right ballpark if you sense your aim as "to be totally open to God." Totally available, all the way down to that innermost point of your being; deeper than your thinking, deeper than your feelings, deeper than your memories and desires, deeper than your usual psychological sense of yourself—even deeper than your presence! For ultimately, what will go on in this prayer is "in secret" (the words Jesus used in his instructions on prayer in Matthew 6:6): deeper than even your conscious mind and your most bedrock sense of "I am here." Hidden even from *yourself*, in that innermost sanctuary of your being—where, in the words of that well-loved monastic formula, your life is "hidden with Christ in God."

Notice that I didn't say that the aim was to make yourself empty or make yourself still. The reason I didn't say so is because it's impossible! Making oneself empty or still does not lie within the capacity of the mind (at least the beginner's mind), and striving for emptiness is a surefire way to guarantee that your meditation will be a constant stream of thoughts.

Empty*ing*, however, is quite another matter—and in fact, brings us right to the heart of what Centering Prayer is all about. We'll see why shortly.

Being clear about your intention is really the touchstone of Centering Prayer, for the method of the prayer will consist primarily of a repeated returning to and refocusing of your intention, just as one repeatedly refocuses a camera lens that has drifted slightly off.

## Putting Teeth in Your Attention

"The road to hell is paved is paved with good intentions," the old cliché goes, and it aptly describes the experience of nearly everyone who begins to work with Centering Prayer. You'll sit down on your prayer stool with the lofty intention of making yourself totally available to God, sincerely wishing to offer up your being in the way just described. And then, not twenty seconds later, you'll catch yourself deeply embroiled in some mental or emotional scenario: replaying that argument you had with your teenager this morning, pondering what to cook for dinner tonight, or whether you remembered to lock the storage bin. Ah, monkey mind! And you'll wonder how you got there, and whatever became of that "naked intent direct to God."

The method of Centering Prayer begins with the reassurance that all this is perfectly normal. Unlike the more concentrative forms of meditation, no effort is made to try to hold the mind firmly and unwaveringly to its goal. Instead, Centering Prayer proposes a simple and elegant solution to the problem of monkey mind. If the term is not too crass, you might think of it in terms of a little "deal" you make with yourself. The deal is this: *If you catch yourself thinking, you let the thought go.*

It's as simple as that. You're not responsible for the thoughts you don't catch (at least not at first; I'll offer some refinements to this instruction a bit later). And you don't need to torment yourself with the question of "Who or what 'catches' itself thinking?" Just deal with what's on your plate, which will be more than enough to keep you busy. If you find yourself tangled up with a thought—no matter what kind of thought—you simply, gently let that thought go. You release it, thus bringing yourself back into alignment with your original intention, which was to maintain that bare, formless openness to God.

Of course, the next thought may be right back, reducing the duration of your bare, formless openness to not much more than a nanosecond. But that's not the point. What *is* the point is beautifully suggested in the following story, now legendary among teachers and practitioners of Centering Prayer. In one of the very earliest training workshops, led by Thomas Keating, a nun tried out her first twenty-minute taste of Centering Prayer and then lamented, "Oh, Father Thomas, I'm such a failure at this prayer. In twenty minutes, I've had ten thousand thoughts."

"How lovely!" responded Thomas Keating without missing a beat. "Ten thousand opportunities to return to God!"

This simple story captures the essence of Centering Prayer. It is meditation based entirely on return—ten thousand times, if it comes to that. We put teeth in our intention to be deeply open to God by our willingness, when we find ourselves "caught out" with a thought, simply to let that thought go. Letting go of a thought is a small but powerful symbol of our willingness in a larger sense to let go of our own stuff and return to that open attending upon God. I sometimes call Centering Prayer "boot camp in Gethsemane," for it practices over and over, thought by thought, the basic gesture of Jesus' night of struggle in the garden: "Not my will be done, Oh Lord, but thine."

This key aspect of Centering Prayer is good news, of course, for those who have struggled long and fruitlessly to establish a meditation practice and have been derailed, like that nun, by the endless stream of thoughts. Centering Prayer is in this sense a totally "win/win" situation. Whatever your mind serves you up is just fine. If you sink immediately into such depths of stillness that when the bowl bell is rung at the end of twenty minutes, it seems like only a minute, great! You've had an easy and blessed time of it. If every minute feels like twenty and you've been bedeviled by thoughts more prolific than the heads of Medusa, but still you've been doing your best to let them go and return to the openness, great! You've gotten a good aerobic workout of your "muscle" of surrender!

Later on, I'll attempt to show how the remark I just made is not a metaphor. Something inside us *is* objectively strengthened by this patient willingness to let go of our own stuff, to do the practice in the face of almost unbearable psychological frustration. We'll see what that "something" is in due course. For the moment, it's enough simply to reiterate Thomas Keating's reassurance that "the only thing you can do wrong in this prayer is to get up and walk out." To sit there and quietly continue to do the practice, even if you perceive your efforts as totally unsuccessful, is, in his words, to know what it means to "consent to the presence and action of God within us" in whatever form it comes. The power of this prayer lies in the consent.

## The Sacred Word

If you've made it to this point in the instructions, you've basically learned the whole method of Centering Prayer. But to make the method a bit easier to apply, a final nuance is added. Normally, in Centering Prayer, this release of a thought is accomplished with the help of what is known as a sacred word.

A sacred word is a word you yourself choose that symbolizes your willingness to "do the deal." It's the spiritual equivalent of a little piece of red string tied around your finger. It helps jog your memory, reminding you simply and promptly to let go of whatever thought you're thinking and return to that "naked intent direct to God."

Depending on your temperament, you might be drawn to a word with clear devotional or religious intent: a word such as "Jesus," "Father," "Abba" (Jesus' own word for opening to the Divine Source in prayer), "Spirit," "Kyrie," or "Come, Lord" (of course, that's a short phrase, but a short phrase is quite acceptable as a sacred word so long as it's *very* short). Or you might be more attracted to a word that describes the spiritual attitude you wish to maintain or reminds you of your basic intention. Such "attitude" words might include "open," "still," "be here," "listen," or "let go." Either kind of sacred word is fine. Short is better than long, and simple is better than fancy.

In trying to describe what a sacred word is, it's probably easiest to describe what it is not. First—and somewhat puzzlingly, you might initially think—the sacred word is not a mantra. The reason it is not a mantra is because you don't repeat it constantly; you only use it when you "notice" that you are being attracted to a thought. While the difference may seem academic at first—it may seem to you that you're simply dropping one thought right after another, so the sacred word might *as well* be a mantra—in point of fact, this is not the case. While you can't experience it subjectively, even in those most turbulent periods of prayer, when it seems like one thought on top of another, there are in fact tiny, microscopic pauses when the thoughts drop out and the sacred word also drops out—a state I sometimes refer to as "traveling at the speed of love." These moments don't last long, typically, but no one ever said that the Divine needed a lot of time to touch our innermost being. It's virtually instantaneous. These small nanosecond "gaps" in the stream of consciousness are in fact central to the method of Centering Prayer and a crucial part of its transformative power. A mantra belongs to concentrative meditation practice, and within the context of a surrender practice such as centering prayer it actually slows down progress.

Second, a sacred word is not a "special" word. It does not sum up or describe the height and depth and breadth of your love for God; nor does it say something special about you. It is simply a place-holder, the finger pointing at the moon of your intention. Laying too much emotional baggage on it can get in the way, stimulating thinking rather than helping you to release from it. Your sacred word should be as simple and emotionally neutral as possible.

Third, the sacred word is not a thought-suppressor, or a baseball bat to put down thoughts or replace them with itself. It simply greases the skids of the letting-go motion, helping you to release thoughts promptly and without a lot of interior reactivity.

Time is what gradually makes the sacred word sacred. Over time, through your repeated, patient use of it to actualize your intention, your word lodges itself deeply in your unconscious, and from there it starts to work its sacred magic.

You'll notice to your wonderment during the prayer time that the word pops up spontaneously as soon as you begin thinking. It's not at all what the instructions first led you to believe. From the instructions, the use of the sacred word sounds like a two-step process: 1: "I" "notice" I am thinking (who or what notices, actually?).

2: I "use" my word to let go of the thought.

Actually, "who or what notices" is something in your un-conscious that has been engaged by your willingness to do this prayer in the first place, and the word pops up out of this same mysterious source virtually simultaneously with your willingness to release the thought. Rather than a two-step process, it's a single, unbroken motion.

After a while, you begin to discover yet another added bene-fit of this sacred word: It will sometimes pop up even when you are not in Centering Prayer—right in the middle of your busy life—to bring you back to center when you find yourself getting agitated or ungrounded. I can't recall the number of times I've been caught in traffic jams or airport security lines, my blood pres-sure escalating rapidly, only to have my word sweetly bubble up from the depths to remind me that every moment I'm actually *here*, I'm in the presence of God.

For this reason, it's good to think of your sacred word as a long-term engagement. I've had mine for fifteen years now, and would change it only for a compelling reason such as a huge inte-rior shift, or the direct prompting of the Holy Spirit. Most people experiment a fair bit at the beginning, trying out this word and that word until they find something that clicks. When they do, it often comes "out of left field" with a force and resonance so strong that one can hardly avoid suspecting the Holy Spirit as the chief operative. A woman in one of my groups in British Columbia is a lovely case in point. After wavering back and forth between the word "trust" and the word "love," she watched in astonishment as suddenly they fused themselves into the short phrase "Trust love," which has been her sacred word for more than five years now.

The only hard and fast rule, of course, is not to change your word during the course of a single Centering Prayer period. The reason is pretty obvious: you'll be spending your time thinking ("Am I getting all I can out of 'peace'? Perhaps I should shift to 'Jesus,'" etc. etc.)! Remember that the word itself is neutral. It's your *intention* that makes it sacred.

## The Mechanics of Sitting

In Centering Prayer, the goal is to keep the body "relaxed but alert." We wish to have it as neutral as possible so that it doesn't get in the way, either by calling attention to itself or by falling asleep.

As in most meditation practices, it's good to have your back as straight as possible and your head balanced on your shoulders, neither drooping down nor scrunched up (these are great ways to give yourself a splitting headache!). Basically, it's the same posture you'd be aiming for if you were singing in a choir. This creates the best conditions for staying present and attentive and for allowing your energy to circulate freely within you.

This being said, however, "relaxed but alert" is always measured against the yardstick of your own physical capacity. If you need to prop yourself up to support your back or sit in an overstuffed chair to cushion aching muscles, by all means do so. I've seen many people with back problems do Centering Prayer lying flat on their back!

It doesn't matter whether you sit in a chair or on a mat or prayer stool on the floor. It's your choice. If you're short and have opted for the chair, a small stool or a pillow under your feet helps to keep your knees comfortably horizontal. If you've opted for the floor, a good way to keep your legs from falling asleep is to make sure that your buttocks are always higher than your knees. Your hands rest comfortably on your knees, either face up or face down.

Typically, your eyes are closed. But common sense prevails here. If you find yourself getting drowsy and your head nodding, open your eyes and focus for a few moments; it will bring you right back.

## Putting It All Together

So what does a period of Centering Prayer actually look like? Let's end this chapter with a brief walk-through.

You begin by sitting down in your chair or on your prayer stool, eyes closed, body relaxed. If you wish, you can collect yourself around your intention with a short prayer such as "Into your hands I commend my spirit," or "O God, I am here; O God, you are here"; or by taking a couple of intentional breaths. But Centering Prayer actually begins when you start to "say" your sacred word, repeating it silently, gently, and at first steadily, as a symbol of your willingness to consent to the presence and action of God during this time of prayer.

The next step is the most important in the practice, and also the most difficult to explain. The usual instructions go something like this: "When you notice that you're no longer being attracted to thinking, you let the word go . . ."

But of course, these instructions are self-canceling and have been the bane of many practitioners attempting to get the hang of this prayer. How can you "notice" without thinking? How can you "decide" to drop the word without that itself being a thought?

In actuality, however, there is a simple magic here, again dependent upon that wonderful operative we looked at earlier, the participation of your unconscious. The easiest way to describe what happens might be through a kind of butchered French: *"il se droppe"*; the word simply drops itself out. It's very similar to the process of falling asleep. You can't see the moment you actually drift off to sleep. It simply happens.

It's essentially the same in Centering Prayer. The crucial moment is taken care of. You don't have to "do" it; it happens on its own, programmed right into your original intention to be deeply open to God. You don't notice the moment you stop thinking; what you notice is the moment you *start* thinking again. You find yourself in the midst of a thought and return to your sacred word as a way of returning to that openness. And then another thought comes, and with it, the return to the sacred word . . .

And on and on it goes, for the twenty minutes or so that you do this prayer (twenty minutes is the recommended minimum time for a single sitting). Subjectively, the only parts you'll directly remember are the times of wrestling with thoughts. But in point of fact, these relatively more agitated, "surface of yourself" times have been counterbalanced by times of deep resting at your depths. You won't be able to perceive these directly, of course (the moment you start thinking about them, they're gone). But you'll retain some residual memory of them in an inexplicable sense of refreshment, and sometimes a vivid sense of having been tugged down deep into your own heart, or of having sat at the edge of an incredible intimacy and tenderness.

For this reason, Thomas Keating advises people over and over again not to look for the fruits of this prayer in their subjective experience of it. Centering Prayer is not about accessing sublime states of consciousness or having mystical experiences. The fruits of this prayer are first seen in daily life. They express themselves in your ability to be a bit more present in your life, more flexible and forgiving with those you live and work with, more honest and comfortable in your own being. These are the real signs that the inner depths have been touched and have begun to set in motion their transformative work.

# 4 ⑥ Handling Thoughts during Prayer Time

At this point in our exploration of Centering Prayer it might be helpful to introduce a pair of terms from the classic vocabulary of Christian spirituality that cover the ground we've just been over from a slightly different angle of vision. While they may initially sound formidable, I like them because once understood, they give an immediate and clear handle on what Centering Prayer is all about.

These words are *cataphatic* and *apophatic*.

*Cataphatic* prayer (sometimes also spelled with a k: *kataphatic*) is prayer that makes use of what theologians call our "faculties." It engages our reason, memory, imagination, feelings, and will. These, of course, are the normal human operating systems that connect us to the outer world and to our own interior life. They are the wonderful tools we have been given to make our way in this world and to experience it richly from the perspective of being a unique person with unique gifts to share and a unique relationship to God.

Cataphatic prayer corresponds to what we have earlier described as our "ordinary awareness." It emerges out of and rein-forces that unique sense of egoic selfhood.

Cataphatic prayer is most of what we are about in church. When I described my earliest childhood instruction in prayer as "talking to God," I was describing cataphatic prayer. Virtually all aspects of our usual worship experience—intercessory and litur-gical prayers, celebrating the Eucharist, choral singing, religious and sacred dance, belong to cataphatic prayer. So also do some classic Western forms of "meditation," such as Ignatian, in which meditation means focused, concentrated work with your imagina-tion on a specific topic either personal or theological. To meditate on the Passion of Christ, in this cataphatic sense, would mean to focus intensely on Christ's suffering and death, deepening your connection to this Mystery by inviting your own feelings and life experience to come into play.

*Apophatic* prayer, by contrast, is prayer that does not make use of the faculties; in other words, it bypasses our capacities for reason, imagination, visualization, emotion, and memory. From the perspective of our faculties, this somewhat amorphous state may feel like emptiness or nothingness, and hence you'll often see this kind of prayer described as "formless," or the *via negativa* ("the way of negation"). In point of fact, once a more subtle discrimina-tion begins to develop in us, we learn that apophatic prayer is far from either formless or empty. It, too, makes use of faculties, but ones that are much more subtle than we're used to and which are normally blocked by overreliance on our more usual mental and affective processing modes. These more subtle faculties of percep-tion have traditionally been known in Christian tradition as the "spiritual senses." I will return to them in more detail in the next chapter; as I described earlier, learning to work with them is some-what equivalent to learning to see in the dark.

Because it bypasses our usual mental processes and the sense of selfhood attached to them, apophatic prayer corresponds to what we have earlier described as our "spiritual awareness." It includes various forms of ecstatic and mystical prayer in which egoic perception is transcended. It also includes most forms of meditation as the term is understood in its classic sense, denoting a systematic practice of intentional silence. Centering Prayer clearly belongs to the generic category of apophatic prayer.

It may not seem immediately clear why it's useful to get a handle on Centering Prayer by describing its generic type. But I am continually impressed by how much trouble this actually saves when it comes to understanding Centering Prayer's challenging instructions about the handling of thoughts during prayer time. Only when the radically apophatic nature of Centering Prayer is recognized does it become possible to relax and really allow the prayer to unfold its deepest treasures. Most of the confusion and equivocation that can creep into the teaching of Centering Prayer, I've found, comes from trying to mix the streams—or in other words, from approaching apophatic prayer with a cataphatic mindset.

Many years ago back in Maine I was invited to join a Centering Prayer group led by a very determined and charismatic spiritual director whose operational style was a prime example of this mixing of the waters. Her group would begin with the usual twenty minutes of silent prayer, but at the end of this time she would break silence by going around the circle and asking each person, "What message did God give you during your time of Centering Prayer?"

Certainly this is one way of interpreting "listening to God," but it's clear that cataphatic listening is what this spiritual director had in mind. From the point of view of cataphatic prayer, silence will always tend to appear as an empty vessel into which God pours "content." The purpose of keeping silence, from this perspective, is to be better able to listen to whatever content God may wish to reveal. Whether this is a summons to some particular mission or vocation or the uncovering of some specific psychological truth yielded up from the unconscious, we tend to think of silence as useful primarily as the precondition for the revelation of new insights and directives.

Apophatic prayer has a very different understanding of silence. Silence is not a backdrop for form, and diffuse, open awareness is not an empty chalice waiting to be filled with specific insights and directives. It is its own kind of perceptivity, its own kind of communion. Rather than yielding itself into form, it is more that we yield ourselves into *it*—just as "pieces of cloud dissolve in sunlight," in the wonderful image of the poet Jelaluddin Rumi.[1] What first appears like a "nothing" to us gradually begins to become filled with its own light and intelligence, and this in turn carries us closer to our own hearts and closer to that mysterious place of interpenetration at the heart of all things. This more subtle level of perceptivity can be sustained only when the denser and noisier perceptions of our usual human faculties have fallen silent.

What lies awaiting us at the heart of this "dark silence" of the apophatic realm is beautifully hinted at by Father Tom Francis, a contemporary Trappist monk and teacher of Centering Prayer. Notice how the classic definition of apophatic as "prayer beyond the faculties" furnishes the cornerstone of his insight:

> Centering Prayer insists that the one who prays wishes to meet God as God is, directly, im-mediately—i.e., not mediated by any thought, prayer, reflection, or reading. And so the eyes are closed, the pray-er shuts down completely all the operations of normal consciousness, not allowing any idea, thought, or image. Thus the normal faculties of intellect, imagination, memory, and will are closed down, inoperative, and the person goes to his center, his spirit, his deep and true Self, his personhood, where he is made to the image of God, spirit to Spirit, in a wordless union, communion, the lover with the Beloved (God Triune) beyond all mediations. . . . It could best be called transcendent consciousness for it is the state of being in direct contact with the God who dwells within. Of course, Jesus the incarnate Son of God is the one and only mediator of this encounter, but one must let go of all other mediations. Jesus does his work without the meditator calling upon Him or talking to Him. Let Jesus do his thing and the pray-er do his, that is, total receptivity![2]

In Centering Prayer, then, we leave the cataphatic world and step completely into the apophatic ground, on its own terms. Both the challenge and the opportunity, from the point of view of ordinary consciousness, is to yield ourselves fully into the embrace of the silence rather than "using" the silence to shore up the projects and goals of our ordinary awareness.

## Leaving Thoughts Behind

This distinction becomes crucially important as we settle down to the actual practice of Centering Prayer—because, as we saw in the last chapter, this prayer works almost entirely on the power of intention. If you really are willing to maintain that deep interior openness, releasing each thought as it comes along, then the noticing and letting go of thoughts will happen spontaneously and reliably. Whatever the "something" is deep within your unconsciousness that is engaged by your willingness to yield yourself into the silence will mysteriously remind you when you're tangled up with a thought, and with little or no resistance you'll allow your sacred word to release it.

But if your intention gets fuzzy—i.e., if there is an incomplete willingness to release a thought; if something in you seems more interested in actually *thinking* it—then your Centering Prayer begins to grow punky in the middle, sort of like a rotting woodpile. You'll encounter a lot of daydreaming and a realization, if you're honest with yourself, that you've simply been wasting time, sitting in a kind of smog rather than actually opening to the depths.

For this reason, introductory workshops in Centering Prayer spend a good deal of time going over the types of thoughts that typically present themselves for thinking during a prayer period. The idea is that "forewarned is forearmed." If you enter the prayer aware that certain kinds of thoughts are likely to make a play for your attention, it becomes a lot easier to recognize them and let go of them promptly, without getting entangled.

In the vocabulary of Centering Prayer the word *thought* is used in the broadest possible context. A thought is not just a mental idea; it can also be an emotion, a memory, an interior dialogue or commentary—or just as easily, a physical stimulation like the buzz of a neon light overhead, an itchy nose, or a sudden pain in your back. A thought is anything that pulls you out of open, undifferentiated awareness and captures your attention in a pinpoint focus. Or in other words, it pulls you out of the apophatic and back into the cataphatic.

In one his most colorful teachings Thomas Keating describes this process using the metaphor of boats on a river. The river, as he depicts it, is your consciousness—which is in fact a constantly moving "stream." Down it float boats, i.e., your thoughts. They may be innocent little "kayaks," like a sudden wisp of wondering about whether you left the keys in the car or if tomorrow is the day to put out the trash. Or they may be huge battleships of raw emotion and contentiousness, such as reliving the fight you had with your boss just before you left on retreat. Or maybe they are half-sunken, waterlogged hulls barely above the surface: old hurts and memories from the past. On and on they float, down the river of your consciousness.

In terms of this metaphor, the ideal way to position yourself during the time of Centering Prayer is to imagine yourself as a scuba diver seated on a rock at the bottom of the riverbed. From your watery perch you can look up and see the hulls of the boats passing overhead. And as long as they're simply passing by, that's fine. You don't have to do anything to prevent their coming and going.

The temptation, however, is to get interested in a particular boat, swim up to the surface of the river, and climb on board. In other words, you get caught up in a particular thought. In place of that relaxed, detached attitude that let the boats come and go as they please, you are now being carried downstream yourself!

Centering Prayer teaching enumerates five types of "boats" that typically float by during prayer time. The first of these, woolgathering, or "ordinary thoughts," actually poses little challenge to your willingness to let go if you catch them quickly enough. These are the sorts of vague, meandering, often whimsical thoughts that pop into your head, typically at the beginning of the prayer period when you're still settling down. The mind roams through its lists and categories, perhaps inventorying the contents of your bureau drawer or Palm Pilot, seeing if you can still name the presidents of the United States in order, or your own variation of these mindless daisy-chains of free association. It's rather like a dog turning round and round in his bed before he finally flops down to rest. But the good news is that these thoughts have little emotional attraction, and pretty soon they settle down of their own accord, or else you simply tune them out—like background music in a department store.

Somewhat more challenging are so-called attractive thoughts—the next category—which includes, in fact, both attractive and repulsive thoughts. These are thoughts that come with an emotional hook in them, like fishing lines dangling down into your river of consciousness. You may find yourself reliving that fight you had with your coworker last week (or with your mother forty years ago!)—maybe even coming up with the perfect rejoinder. Or blissfully daydreaming ahead to your upcoming getaway weekend or hiking trip, or savoring a compliment thrown your way. The telltale sign that you've been hooked by an attractive thought is that when that mysterious something "reminds" you of your intention to sit there in open, deep awareness, your first reaction is reluctance—"Well, just let me first finish thinking this thought, then I'll get right back to my Centering Prayer."

## Self-Reflection

The fourth type of thought (and yes, I will get back to the third!) is self-reflection. This is admittedly the *bête noire* of Centering Prayer. Because the prayer works completely with intention rather than attention, it leaves the attention with no specific marching orders—unlike concentrative methods, which furnish the mind with a simple, repetitive task to do like saying the mantra or following the breath. Particularly if you've been trained in an attention-based method, this lack of focal point can be initially maddening. The mind, not knowing what else to put its attention on, begins to put its attention on itself, and a kind of mental mitosis ensues: "Am I in stillness?" "Is this a thought that I'm thinking?" "Who is the inner watcher that notices?" etc. This solipsistic tendency already inherent in Centering Prayer has unfortunately been aggravated by confusing instructions you'll sometimes hear around the word *awareness:* "When you become aware that you're no longer attracted to thinking, it is all right to let the sacred word go," or "When you become aware that you're being attracted to a thought, just let that thought go." Who or what is that "you" that becomes aware, you wonder, and the mind starts twisting around on itself.

The way out of this hall of mirrors is really very simple if you're willing to be firm. There's a basic law of consciousness that states: What you pay attention to, you energize; what you withdraw attention from loses force. If you spend your time watching the watcher, you energize the problem. If you can learn not to pay attention to it, it will eventually subside. What this means is simply to do the practice. Treat self-reflection simply like another kind of thought, and patiently let it go. The cataphatic cannot watch the apophatic; and all the mental mitosis really boils down to the struggle of ordinary awareness not to lose its grip on a process that actually goes on far more naturally without it. Once you see the truth of this, self-reflection begins to lose its hook.

## Thoughts from the Unconscious

The last category is known in Centering Prayer nomenclature as "thoughts from the unconscious." This is the category where you have to apply the word *thought* in its broadest possible context including emotions and sensations, for these are typically what this last category consists of. Sometimes you'll be sitting in prayer and find yourself inexplicably near tears, or even in fact crying! This may strike you as particularly odd because you weren't aware you were sad when you sat down to do the prayer. Or occasionally you'll find yourself in the presence of a spike of emotional or even physical pain: a raw surge of anxiety or anger, or a sudden throbbing muscle or dizziness that wasn't there before you sat down to do the prayer. You wonder what's going on, whether you're going crazy.

What's going on is that the relaxed, gentled attention of Centering Prayer is allowing some interior rearrangement to go on. We all carry a lot of pain deep inside us, buried in our emotions and in our bodies. Through your willingness to "consent to the presence and action of God," the tight repressive bands that the egoic mind keeps wrapped around these shadow places within you begin to loosen up, and some of the trapped material can release itself, most often in tears. While this may initially feel disconcerting, it is actually a sign that a process of inner healing is under way.

Without doubt, herein lies Thomas Keating's most profound contribution to contemporary spiritual psychology: in his recognition that Centering Prayer in some mysterious but undeniable way helps to initiate a process of psychological healing that he calls "the Divine Therapy." We will be looking at his very important teaching in Part III of this book. For now, it's enough simply to offer the reassurance that this "unloading of the unconsciousness" as it's sometimes known in Centering Prayer circles is all perfectly normal and typically quite gentle—so gentle that most people in the early stages of learning the prayer do not notice it at all.

## The Art of Letting Go

The goal in Centering Prayer is not to stop the thoughts, but simply to develop a detached attitude toward them. As long as they are coming and going of their own accord, there is no need to be constantly repeating your Sacred Word. The Word is only used to help you jump off the boat and swim back down to your little diver's rock once you realize you've been caught.

In introductory Centering Prayer workshops this gentle, laissez-faire attitude toward the thoughts is reinforced through a simple formula called "The Four Rs":

Resist no thought

Retain no thought

React to no thought

Return to the sacred word

*Resist no thought* means just that. According to scientific research, the stream of consciousness is constantly moving along, and without specialized training it is nearly impossible for most people to keep their mind on a single thought for more than two minutes. The good news in this is that by the time a thought emerges into consciousness, it's already on the way out! If you don't feed it with commentary or reaction, it will soon enough move on of its own accord.

*Retain no thought* is the other side of the same coin: "You catch yourself thinking, you let the thought go." It is the willingness to "do the deal," as I described it in the last chapter: to let go of any thought promptly and without reluctance.

*React to no thought* means to let go of the thought without internal commentary or self-criticism, which so often merely results in turning an innocent thought into an emotionally charged scenario. "What, I'm still getting snagged on self-reflection!" or "How could such a violent thought have emerged from me? What kind of monster am I, anyway?" An emotionally charged thought is a lot harder to let go than a simple woolgathering or daydream.

*Return to the sacred word* means simply to say your word again (or allow it to say itself) as a symbol of your willingness to release whatever the particular thought may be and return to your state of open awareness. Thomas Keating emphasizes that this release should be extremely gentle; in fact, Centering Prayer trainees learn this last "R" phrase as "return *ever-so-gently* to your sacred word."

## Simultaneity

While it's hard to describe exactly *how* this happens, it is quite normal in Centering Prayer to know that thoughts are going on, but to know as well that you have absolutely no attraction to them. It's as if two scenarios are going on at once, but you honestly know that the activity at the surface is in no way disrupting your quietly gathered being at the depths. For as long as this state of simultaneity lasts, it's fine to let it be, but if the balance shifts and the surface begins to exert its attraction, simply allow your Sacred Word to return you to those apophatic depths.

If you're doing the practice of Centering Prayer faithfully and consistently, letting go of the thoughts as you notice them, not worrying too much and not getting too tangled up in self-reflection, what you are actually patterning into yourself is a very important piece of spiritual learning: that access to the apophatic realm is somehow related to this act of letting go—or *surrender,* to give it its true spiritual name. This is a profoundly important insight whose implications we'll explore more deeply in the next chapter.

# 5 ⑥ Spiritual Non-Possessiveness

Let's return now to the third category, which I skipped over in the last chapter because it poses the most serious challenges for those approaching Centering Prayer from traditional Christian cataphatic starting points. This third category is known in Centering Prayer teaching as "insights and illuminations"—to which I add a third tempter: "intercessions."

I spoke earlier about the group leader in Maine who closed each session of Centering Prayer with the question "And what message did God give you during your time of Centering Prayer?" It is a deep and persistent proclivity of our Judeo-Christian tradition to regard silence as a backdrop for listening for messages. In fact, that is what "listening to God" will normally connote. We think of Abraham and Moses or the long line of Old Testament prophets who went out into bare and stony places to receive messages about what they were to do next. And it is hard to erase this cataphatic programming from our hearts and our expectations.

So you'll be sitting in Centering Prayer, and suddenly out of that luminous openness something will begin to emerge into form.

43

It may be an insight, either psychological or spiritual. Perhaps the key sentence you need for that sermon you've been working on will pop into your mind. Or you'll suddenly understand a piece of your psychological past that has always eluded you: where your fear of heights came from, or why you get so enraged when you perceive yourself being undercut. Or perhaps the discernment you've been waiting for about whether to say yes or no to that new job opportunity is suddenly there for you.

This illumination can also be deeply devotional or mystical. Sometimes there are visions, or dazzling visual fragments: Jesus reaching out a hand to you, or a shimmering golden mandala, or gently swirling colors. Or suddenly, out of nowhere, you'll find yourself stirred to pray for everyone you know and begin silently reciting their names, or the words of the Lord's Prayer or the Hail Mary.

As you sit there surrounded by all that blessedness, the instructions of Centering Prayer—"When you catch yourself thinking, you let the thought go"—seem not only harsh, but plain old *wrong*. Isn't this the mother lode? Isn't this what silence is actually for: to bring us into the rich presence of God where we can receive the "daily bread" that God intends for us?

So it is important to be very, very clear as to why those seemingly harsh instructions of Centering Prayer are not only correct but in fact crucial, and to offer reassurances that what is seemingly lost in the letting go—even if it seems like letting go of the pot of gold at the end of the rainbow—is more than compensated for by what is found. Centering Prayer is based on very sound apophatic theology, and if you're really willing to trust it, it will take you all the way there.

First, a very practical reassurance: Don't worry—any genuine insights or messages revealed during Centering Prayer will be back in conscious form. Apophatic prayer is sacred space for God as well as human beings, and the divine does not use this space to play striptease with us! Typically, an insight or message that is emerging from the unconscious into your conscious attention will make its way up as inexorably as crabgrass growing through the tarmac. It will visit you not only in your prayer time but also in your dreams, and your conscious mind will be able to retrieve it after the prayer time. You don't have to grab onto it during your Centering Prayer; if it's real, it will be back.

Conversely, many of the insights and visions that seem so compelling to us in prayer time turn out to be chimera: just like dreams that seem so real to us while we're dreaming them, but we awake to say, "Well, what was *that* all about?"

Throughout this entire category of insights, illuminations, and intercessions, we have to suspect that the principal operative is really the old cliché "The ego abhors a vacuum." From the point of view of ordinary (or cataphatic) awareness, the apophatic will always appear to be a vacuum, and your ego will incessantly try to fill up this vacuum with content. If you grab onto an insight or illumination, or succumb to the temptation to pray for everyone then and there, what you have actually done is to allow yourself to be dragged out of the apophatic back into the cataphatic. Contemplative teaching—at least the most authentic and powerful of contemplative teaching—emphasizes that this is never worth the price.

Why? What lessons are to be learned by staying with the apophatic? Here is the answer from Christian contemplative tradition, which you will find affirmed by all the great mystics, from John of the Cross and *The Cloud of Unknowing* in medieval times through Thomas Keating and Thomas Merton in our own: By your willingness to stay with the apophatic at all costs during the time of this prayer (and remember, we're only concerned with what goes on during the twenty minutes or so you're doing Centering Prayer; you are perfectly welcome to do intercessory prayer afterwards) you are strengthening and deepening an attitude of soul that will protect you and carry you all the way: the attitude of spiritual non-possessiveness.

### "Blessed are the poor in spirit . . ."

So what is spiritual non-possessiveness, anyway? Jesus' very first words in the Beatitudes—"Blessed are the poor in spirit, for theirs is the Kingdom of Heaven"—suggest the centrality of this quality to his teaching and to his life. He touches it again during that first temptation in the wilderness in his determination not to turn stones into bread, and still again during his arrest and crucifixion through his refusal to rescue himself.[1] The same quality is captured in the traditional monastic vows of poverty, chastity, and obedience, and in the traditional Buddhist teaching "Try to develop a mind that clings to nothing."

Our natural inclination, or course, is to grab on: to help ourselves and build ourselves up. "Spiritual materialism" is the name that Tibetan Buddhist master Trungpa Rinpoche gave to this attitude nearly four decades ago. Basically, it means the tendency to help ourselves to spiritual experience in order to build up our cataphatic, or ordinary, self. If time spent in those apophatic depths yields up new information about ourselves, we want to quickly get it all down in our journal. Or if it gives us wonderful experiences of intimate presence with God—what John of the Cross calls "spiritual consolations"—we want to savor them and allow them to deepen our own trust and sense of being specially loved by God.

What's so bad about that?

Well, nothing, initially. And in fact, at a certain stage in our spiritual practice, when we are just setting out on the contemplative path, or when we're feeling wounded or unsure of ourselves, it may be exactly what is needed. But it is an immature stage of practice, something like a crutch. While the leg is broken, the crutch is useful for helping us get around, but if we hang onto it after the leg is healed, it really slows us down. If we do not grow beyond the attitude of spiritual materialism, it leaves us with some very different habits to unlearn. And if we really can't or won't leave the cataphatic safety zone, it will eventually limit the level of selfhood we are able to realize to the egoic self and make the unitive consciousness that we taste and yearn for impossible to sustain.

Here are the two pertinent teachings from contemplative tradition.

## 1. Disciplining the Imagination

In our Western culture, imagination is almost universally and indiscriminately assumed to be a good thing, and much of what we call "creativity" includes encouraging the mind to shake itself free and roam where it will. But in the classic spiritual teachings of our Christian tradition, the desert fathers and mothers of the third through sixth centuries spent much time struggling with the imagination and taught emphatically that it is only through the imagination that the demonic can gain access! Temptation can only enter us, contemplative tradition insists, through our fantasies, daydreams, and *logismoi* (the desert fathers' words for "thoughts" or trains of commentaries). If we can learn to simply say "no" to these, not take the bait, there is no way that the "passions" (fear, envy, anger, pride, etc.) can get hold of us.

I confess that I didn't fully understand what this meant until I read *The Tibetan Book of Death and Dying*, which became a bestseller about a decade ago and helped many Westerners to discover the truth in their own tradition in a much deeper way.[2] According to Tibetan Buddhist tradition, when a person dies, they have an immediate opportunity to recognize the "clear luminosity" that shines all around them as their own true nature. If they miss this opportunity, a second chance emerges. That clear luminous light will begin to break up into colors, and the colors will begin to swirl and take on feeling tones, such as hope, desire, or fear. If the person gets fascinated with these color patterns and begins to interact with the emotions they suggest, he or she will be "hooked," and dragged down into another cycle of death and rebirth. If the person can simply stay clear and realize that all the swirling colors, emotions, and forms are just a dissolution of the original white light, then he or she will have a second and in some ways even more profound opportunity to escape from the wheel of rebirth.

Of course, Christianity looks on death and the hereafter in a very different way, but the teaching itself is analogous to the situation in Centering Prayer. Our job when we enter the waters of apophatic prayer is to stay with the unity, with the clear light. If

47

we allow it to become refracted into images, colors, and feeling tones, we will be whisked back into our psychological self, with its endless wheel of emotions, agendas, and reactions.

It's important to note that this is exactly the opposite of the teaching you sometimes hear in Christian fundamentalist circles: "The devil will get you if you make your mind a blank." To begin with, as we've already noted, apophatic consciousness is a far cry from making your mind a blank. But the main point is that it's only when we *start* thinking that evil or the demonic can insinuate itself into our consciousness, for its entry point is always by using the imagination to stir up those emotional reactions. Fundamentalists tend to be wary of those sometimes swirling and dark thoughts that emerge from the shadow side of our being and from the human libido itself. Their strategy is to keep a strong hold on the conscious mind, using the superego to suppress the unconscious. But Centering Prayer teaches a much kinder, gentler, and more time-tested way: we can allow anything to come up out of the unconsciousness, and it will have absolutely no hold on us as long as we are willing to let go of it. If we don't grab it, it can't grab us. Whatever the Christian equivalent may be of the Tibetan Buddhist scenario of the clear luminosity, it is utterly true that the practice of not clinging to the creations of the imagination will allow us to stand deeply and quietly gathered in the heart of God, no matter what outer or inner storms may assail us.

## 2. Moving beyond the Experience/Experiencer Dualism

Self-reflexive consciousness, you remember from our earlier discussion, works through the subject/object polarity, and our usual sense of self emerges from this polarity. From our usual vantage point, it appears that we "have" spiritual experiences, which then contribute to "our" insight, illumination, and eventually full enlightenment. From this perspective, more is better, and enlightenment looks quantitative: when we've acquired "enough" silence, stability, concentration, spiritual experience, we will emerge into the final stage of our human personhood, traditionally called in

Christianity the "unitive" stage, or "transforming union."

But the trap in this scenario is that dualistic-based selfhood cannot possibly attain unitive consciousness. It's an oxymoron, like a two-wheeled tricycle! As long as we operate out of the subject-object polarity of self-reflexive consciousness, we will continue to pile up spiritual experiences, but we are halted at what tradition calls the "illuminative stage," a stage which the contemporary mystic Evelyn Underhill once likened to "basking like a pious tabby in the light of the divine."[3] Ultimately, we cannot have our cake and eat it too, and to step into full unitive consciousness requires letting go of that lesser consciousness which would prefer to revel in its own experience.

To arrive at this unified whole, there is only one route to get there, and it is known to all the spiritual traditions of the world: dying to self. The self who "has" experiences must finally be let go, as consciousness steps out into the bare, positionless freedom which is unity. And when all the theological rhetoric has been pared away, dying to self looks remarkably similar to that simple gesture, practiced over and over in Centering Prayer, of letting it go, giving it away. One does not "snatch" at insights, illuminations, experiences, because the only known route to unitive freedom is in the dying, in the moving not toward more, but toward less. The greatest of all spiritual teachers have always known this, and the lesser have always tried to qualify it. It is easy to fall into the trap of thinking that one dies to the lesser in order to "gain" the greater. But the great spiritual teachers (of which Jesus was clearly among the greatest-of-the-great) do not say that. You do not die on a cross *in order* to "set up" the resurrection; you die on a cross because the willingness to give it all away is itself the original and ultimate creative act from which all being flows.

Ultimately, this is the final and sometimes painful course correction that lies in wait at the end of a long road of spiritual practice with more concentrative meditation methods. Over time, with sincerity and dedication, it is possible to become proficient at holding the mind at a single point and accessing quite profound and powerful states of bliss and clarity. We can "have" what we want. And so the last attachment must be broken: the attachment to *having* itself. A poem by the great Indian mystic Rabindranath Tagore depicts this painful "stuck" place with harrowing honesty:

> Time after time
> I came to your gate with raised hands,
> Asking for more and yet more.
> You gave and gave, now in slow measure, now
> In sudden excess.
> I took some, and some things I let drop; some
> Lay heavy on my hands;
> Some I made into playthings and broke them
> When tired;
> Till the wrecks and hoards of your gifts grew
> Immense, hiding you, and the ceaseless
> Expectation wore my heart out.
> Take, oh take—has now become my cry.
> Shatter all from this beggar's bowl:
> Put out the lamp of the importunate
> Watcher.
> Hold my hands, raise me from the
> Still-gathering heap of your gifts
> Into the bare infinity of your uncrowded
> Presence.[4]

Put very simply, Centering Prayer avoids this steep and painful place in the learning curve by not patterning the habit of spiritual acquisitiveness in the first place. From the start one learns to recognize and prefer the simple act of release to whatever could be had by holding on. The value of this training becomes increasingly obvious as one's journey converges toward center.

## The Apophatic Self

Just as cataphatic awareness reinforces a cataphatic sense of self, so apophatic awareness connects us up to an apophatic sense of self. The act of recognizing and trusting this connection is usually the crucial turning point in the struggle to let go of insights and illuminations. As long as it feels to us as if apophatic prayer is simply sitting there in darkness, we will not be able to directly experience why it is virtuous to do so, and the temptation to hang on to "juicy" thoughts will remain.

Gradually though, after repeated practice in following the instructions, taking them on faith, as it were, the Mystery begins to reveal itself: The apophatic darkness is neither "dark" nor "empty" nor "formless." Rather, it is the core of our own true perceptivity. It is filled with subtle perceptive faculties—the spiritual senses, as they're known in Christian mystical tradition[5]—and a kind of intuitive hologram knowingness which is the core motion of unitive consciousness and the foundation of unitive selfhood. Once this truth begins to be glimpsed, apophatic practice ceases to be a burden and begins to sparkle with the joy of discovery and imminence of encounter. "In the center of one's nothingness one meets the infinitely real," says Thomas Merton, adding,

> This act of total surrender is not merely a fantastic intellectual and mystical gamble; it is something much more serious. It is an act of love for this unseen person, who, in the very gift of love by which we surrender ourselves to his reality also makes his presence known to us.[6]

Call that "unseen person" Christ, God, or one's own deepest self: The path of surrender practiced in each tiny letting go eventually fills in the darkness with the intimate knowledge of the face we had before we had a face, the oneness in love which is the way of "knowing in being known."

# PART II

## The Tradition of Centering Prayer

# 6 ⑥ Centering Prayer and Christian Tradition

C entering Prayer, along with its sister discipline, Christian Meditation, made its appearance in the modern Christian world in the mid-1970s. Since this was also the era of that first grand arrival of Eastern spiritual paths on North American shores, you'll sometimes hear the argument (mostly from Christians who were never exposed to contemplative prayer in the Christianity they grew up with) that meditation is not intrinsically Christian, but simply an effort to graft Eastern practices onto Western spirituality. Centering Prayer, you'll sometimes hear it said, is just "a Christianized TM."[1]

If this assertion is true, it's curious, then, that the three names most widely associated with the recent popularization of meditation in the Christian West—Thomas Merton, Thomas Keating, and John Main—have in common the fact that they are all Benedictine monks (two of them abbots), with considerable spiritual maturity and contemplative experience under their belts. Thomas Merton, in so many ways the great spiritual pioneer of our times, as early as the early 1960s was writing books calling for such a recovery of contemplative prayer not only within the monastery but *beyond* it.

Thomas Keating and John Main essentially responded to his prophetic call, developing simple meditation methods solidly rooted in Christian spiritual tradition and suitable for use not only within the cloister walls, but in a world hungry for the recovery of its spiritual roots. All three of these men recognized meditation not as a newfangled innovation, let alone the grafting onto Christianity of an alien tradition, but rather, as something that had originally been at the very center of Christian practice and had become lost.[2]

In the case of Centering Prayer, Thomas Keating tells the following story about how Centering Prayer came to be developed at St. Joseph's Abbey, the Trappist monastery in Spencer, Massachusetts, where for twenty years he served as abbot. A few miles down the road from the abbey, a former Catholic retreat house had closed down and been sold to a Buddhist group. When the facility reopened as the Insight Meditation Center (it's still very much alive today, teaching the path of Vipassana, or Insight Meditation), suddenly the monks at St. Joseph's began to notice an increase of people, almost inevitably young people, stopping by the monastery guest house—asking for directions about how to get to the Insight Meditation Center! Dismayed but intrigued, Keating began to engage some of these young pilgrims in dialogue. What was it they were seeking at the Insight Meditation Center? To which the response nearly always came, in the vernacular of the Sixties, "A path, man! We're seeking a path." Discovering that the vast majority of these seekers had been raised as Christians, he asked the sixty-four-dollar question—"So, why don't you search for a path within your own tradition?" To which he received the genuinely astonished answer, "You mean Christianity has a *path*??"

These young seekers knew what they wanted, and whatever they may or may not have been taught in their religious upbringing, they instinctively knew what a path was: a meditation-based practice that actually changed the way you perceived reality and lived your life. In all their young years as Christians somehow this most crucial part of the Christian message had not gotten through.

Frustrated, Keating took his perceptions to the chapter meeting, the weekly gathering of the monastic community, and issued the following challenge: "Is it not possible to put the essence of the Christian contemplative path into a meditation method accessible to modern people living in the world?" These Trappist monks knew full well that Christianity had a rich and deep contemplative path: They had been living it all their adult lives. But how to share this treasure with young Christians, who seemed to be defecting wholesale to eastern meditation practices?

One of the monks took Keating up on the challenge: Father William Meninger, now a monk at St. Benedict's Monastery in Snowmass, Colorado, and the official "founder" of the method of Centering Prayer. And Father Meninger knew exactly where to look. He took out his well-thumbed copy of *The Cloud of Unknowing*, a fourteenth-century spiritual classic by an anonymous English monk, a book he claims to have read more than 150 times! There, in Chapter Seven, he found the following instructions:

> For this reason, whenever you feel yourself drawn to devote yourself to this work, and whenever you feel by grace that you have been called to do it, lift up your heart toward God with a meek stirring of love. And understand by God the God who made you and formed you and who has graciously called you to your present degree; and do not accept in your mind any other conception of God. And not even all of this is necessary, but only if you are so inclined, for a naked intent direct to God is sufficient without anything else.
>
> And if you desire to have this aim concentrated and expressed in one word in order that you might be better able to grasp it, take but one short word of a single syllable. This is better than two, for the shorter it is the better it accords with the work of the spirit. Such a word is the word GOD or the word LOVE. Choose whichever one you prefer, or, if you like, choose another than suits your taste, provided that it is one syllable. And clasp this word tightly in your heart so that it never leaves it no matter what may happen.[3]

Those paragraphs became the cornerstone of the method of Centering Prayer. To create an "updated format" (as Thomas Keating refers to it), the monks borrowed some of the external trappings from Eastern meditational methods: the convention of group meditation itself (monks had traditionally done their contemplative prayer alone in their cells) and an official beginning and ending time, signaled by a prayer or a bell. Beginning in about 1975, the monks started to offer this simple method of meditation to retreatants at St. Joseph's Abbey. At first, in fact, it was called "Prayer of the Cloud," but the phrase "Centering Prayer," originally coined by Thomas Merton, seemed to offer a more inviting description. The practice caught on, particularly among lay retreatants, and has grown steadily ever since. Today, thousands of people practice Centering Prayer worldwide, supported by an international membership network known as Contemplative Outreach, which provides regular opportunities for teaching and practice.[4]

In the Christian faith, authority is generally recognized as being conveyed through three streams: Scripture, Doctrine, and Tradition. Of these three, the strongest current of authority for the inherent "Christian-ness" of Centering Prayer runs through the stream of tradition, particularly Benedictine monastic tradition. While *The Cloud of Unknowing* is the immediate source for Centering Prayer, *The Cloud* itself rests on a stream of lived tradition by then more than a thousand years old.

In a short summary, which is the most this chapter can be, it's obviously impossible to overview the entire history of Christian spiritual practice. But the lineage of Centering Prayer, from its headwaters in the spiritual teachings and practice of Jesus himself down into our own times, rests on two major stepping stones: the spiritual practice of the Desert Fathers and Mothers in the third through sixth centuries, and the Benedictine tradition of praying the scriptures known as *lectio divina*. Let's look at each of these in turn.

## Meeting the Contemplative Jesus

It would make matters hugely simpler, of course, if we could claim any clear, unambiguous scriptural references to substantiate that Jesus either practiced meditation himself or specifically taught it to his disciples. We can't. Even given the huge caveat that our written gospels represent only a small portion of what Jesus actually taught—plus the fact that in virtually every spiritual tradition practice is taught by oral transmission, one-on-one or in small groups, rather than being written down or even spoken publicly—the fact is, we still need to read a lot between the lines.

It seems safe to assume that Jesus was a contemplative, by which I mean that the intentional alternation between contemplation and action is one of the fundamental rhythms of his being. At all the great junctures of his life—in the first temptations in the wilderness, in his withdrawal to the far shores of Lake Galilee immediately preceding the miracle of the loaves and fishes, at his transfiguration on Mt. Tabor and at the final anguish in the garden of Gethsemane—his pattern is to withdraw into solitude to listen more deeply to the word of God and unite his being to the divine Will.[5] Whether this was a cataphatic or an apophatic listening is not specified, of course, but, in the light of Jesus' own deepest self-disclosure, "I and my Father are one" (John 10:30), we know that the place of oneness is touched at the apophatic rather than the cataphatic level, and can, I think, safely assume that the prayer which Jesus prayed in these solitary times and places was an inter-communion of his and his Father's divine consubstantiality rather than a request for discernment or marching orders.

In his teachings on prayer in Matthew 6:5ff., Jesus emphasizes that true prayer is offered "in secret":

> And when you pray, do not be like the hypocrites, for they love to pray standing in the synagogues and on the street corners to be seen by men. . . . But when you pray, go into your room, close the door and pray to your Father, who is unseen. Then your Father, who sees what is done in secret, will reward you.

This text has figured prominently in contemplative teaching from John Cassian in the fifth century right through Thomas Keating, for obvious reasons. Clearly, at a literal level it is talking about motivation in prayer: moving away from an external, egoic sort of prayer, whose major agenda is to have oneself perceived by others as devout, into a sincerity of heart that is shared between oneself and God alone. But if the text is taken metaphorically—and Jesus himself gives us fair warning that his teachings are indeed intended to be heard more subtly by "those who have ears"—the passage gives a perfectly accurate description of the actual method of apophatic prayer, or meditation. "Go into your room and close the door" would correspond to entering that "cave of your heart" (as the desert fathers would later dub it) and closing the door to "the faculties," or ordinary awareness. "Your Father who is in secret" suggests a being-to-being communion in that apophatic band of receptivity, hidden from the prying gaze of our outer faculties and gathered in the heart of divine love, which is in fact reward in itself, as the passage suggests. This second, more metaphoric, interpretation is specifically invited by Cassian himself, and its legitimacy finds further confirmation in the fact that "prayer in secret" is a recognized category in Near Eastern tradition. In later Sufi texts (which build on the spiritual foundation of Syriac Christianity, the most immediate repository of Jesus' own lived tradition and teaching), the term refers specifically to prayer that is hidden from the outer faculties.[6] This fascinating textual clue brings us as close as we can possibly get to the missing desideratum: scriptural evidence that Jesus both practiced and taught a form of meditation.[7]

## Following Jesus into the Desert

By the early fourth century, as the Christian Church found itself suddenly catapulted from forbidden cult to imperial religion, a significant and growing remnant of Christians experienced this sudden catapult into ecclesiastical stardom as posing a barrier to the authentic practice of their faith. Preferring the more solitary landscape of Jesus' own most intimate practice of prayer, they entered the deserts of Egypt and Syria first in trickles, then in steady streams, tugged by a homing instinct as surely as salmon swimming upstream. Their teachings and practices furnish the curriculum of Christianity's first and in some ways still most influential school of inner awakening.

Until relatively recently the actual legacy of these teachings remained unknown to everyday Christians, sealed away in a forbidding set of Latin volumes called the *Patrologia Latina*, found mostly in monastic or seminary libraries and rarely opened even there. Most of the popular information that managed to trickle out about these earliest Christian monastics was of the *Ripley's Believe It or Not* variety: filled with stereotypes of God-intoxicated fanatics performing bizarre ascetic feats in order to gain their reward in the next life.

That impression began to change in 1964 when Thomas Merton published a marvelous little book called *The Wisdom of the Desert*. Accurately perceiving that the desert masters were not body-hating, world-denying fanatics but remarkably well-grounded spiritual masters, much like the Zen masters of ancient and contemporary times, he made their actual teachings available for the first time in a contemporary, accessible way. Following in Merton's wake, the next decade or so brought a spate of excellent new translations and commentaries that have opened up the tradition in whole new ways and provided modern seekers with a fresh glimpse of what spiritual practice was actually like in those first centuries of Christianity. The recovery of this desert wisdom has been a real inner-eye opener.

When it comes to piecing together the actual prayer and meditation practices of the desert monks, we could characterize their life overall as an attempt to live out fully St. Paul's exhortation to "pray without ceasing" through the discipline of living in constant remembrance of God. The cornerstone, both in prayer and in daily life, was the practice of attention. In daily life, where a monk earned his keep through simple chores such as plaiting rope, the goal was to learn to keep one's mind entirely on what one was doing, without the intrusion of fantasy, daydreaming, or inner commentaries. The same was true of prayer, as this vivid vignette from teachings of St. Anthony makes clear:

> When the holy Abba Anthony lived in the desert he was beset by *accidie* and attacked by many sinful thoughts. He said to God, "Lord, I want to be saved but these thoughts do not leave me alone; what shall I do in my affliction? How shall I be saved?" A short while afterwards when he got up to go out, Anthony saw a man like himself sitting down and plaiting a rope, then getting up again to pray. It was an angel of the Lord sent to correct and reassure him. He heard the angel say, "Do this and you will be saved."[8]

When you're working, work; when you're praying, pray. This was the message of the angel, as it has been of all great spiritual teachers and masters of the art of presence. The practice of intentional silence (as I described it in Chapter 1) is exactly this, the learning to confine the mind within the present moment without allowing it to wander. Attention is certainly the foundational skill of all meditation, and it is clearly the foundation of desert spirituality.

As to specific disciplines of prayer, these desert pioneers worked mostly with the psalms, and with such an intensity of commitment that later monastic tradition remembers them as having chanted the entire psalter—all 150 psalms—as a daily practice![9] While this may be a bit of an exaggeration, it is clear that the psalms were the mainstay of the desert devotional life. And that this chanting was supposed to be an *intentional* practice, not merely a mindless recitation, is clear from a number of reminders scattered throughout the desert writings such as the following:

> It is a great thing to pray without distraction, but to chant psalms without distraction is even greater.[10]

From clues such as these we can characterize the basic spiritual training of the desert as foundational work in the practice of attention based on the chanting of the psalms, undergirded by an inner attitude of humility and surrender that could be counted on to come to one's assistance when all else failed. How should one pray? As Abba Macarius teaches, in what could well be seen as a fourth-century forerunner of Centering Prayer:

> There is no need to make long discourses; it is enough to stretch out one's hands and say, "Lord, as you will and as you know, have mercy." And as the conflict grows fiercer, say, "Lord, help!"[11]

## A Cautionary Note, However . . .

But while the Desert Fathers clearly practiced intentional silence, I am myself not comfortable in moving from this to the assumption that they therefore taught meditation per se—at least in the form that it is now understood and taught in both Centering Prayer and Christian Meditation. This is the assumption made by John Main, the founder of Christian Meditation, when he searched the teachings of the fifth-century desert master John Cassian and found there what he believed to be an explicit reference to the practice of meditation. In the passage in question (the Tenth Spiritual Conference) Cassian recommends as a means to attaining continuous attention in prayer the repeated use of a versicle from Psalm 70: "Oh God, come to my assistance, Oh Lord make haste to help me." Describing this as a practice "which has been handed on to some of us by the oldest of the Fathers," he stresses its powerful efficacy: "This short verse is an indomitable wall for those struggling against the onslaught of demons. It is an impenetrable breastplate and the sturdiest of shields."[12]

"Aha, a mantra!" John Main concluded, and in his teachings on Christian Meditation he has subsequently referred to it as such, giving the impression that the Desert Fathers actually used the word *mantra* and specifically sanctioned and taught a practice of meditation.

But there is one small catch, evident in the sentences immediately following, which are always deleted in John Main's commentaries. For Cassian goes on to explain:

It is not without good reason that this verse has been chosen from the whole of scripture as a device. *It carries within it all the feelings of which human nature is capable. . . .* It carries within it a cry to God in the face of every danger. It expresses the humility of a pious confession. It conveys the watchfulness born of unending worry and fear. It conveys a sense of our frailty, the assurance of being heard, the confidence in help that is always and everywhere present. . . . This is the voice filled with the ardor of love and charity. This is the terrified cry of someone who sees the snares of the enemy, the cry of someone besieged day and night and exclaiming that he cannot escape unless his protector comes to his rescue.[13]

In other words, while it is certainly true that Cassian is describing intentional silence, it is also clear that he is describing *cataphatic* rather than apophatic prayer. While the phrase "O God, come to my assistance, O Lord make haste to help me" superficially resembles a mantra, it is not *used* as a mantra—i.e., as a way of tethering the mind so as to bypass ordinary thinking. Rather, it is intended to work with the feelings—much more like the *zikr* of Sufi ecstatic prayer, or the Jesus Prayer of later Orthodox tradition—so concentrating and intensifying the feelings that they actually "implode" into that level of deeper spiritual awareness. This method is called "bringing the mind down into the heart," and it is the classic path in both the Christian East and the Christian West for passing from the cataphatic to the apophatic.

While this may seem like a nuance, it is a fairly important one. In his attempt to find a solid contextual grounding for meditation in Christian tradition, I believe that Dom Main has slightly shifted the sense of this passage and hence its solid fidelity to the classical tradition of Christian contemplative prayer. In classic Christian practice one does not immediately access the apophatic by simply tethering the faculties; one takes the more circuitous route of concentrating them and intensifying them until they are finally overwhelmed in the divine love. Eventually, of course, one comes out in the same place: in the complete transcendence of the egoic realm and the opening of one's heart to become "all flame."[14]

It's probably safer simply to concede that Christian Meditation and Centering Prayer are slightly innovative in terms of the classical tradition; they represent a definite expansion and development of the traditional methodology of contemplative prayer. It is a development, I believe, that is theologically compatible with the tradition and has in fact been implicit in the tradition for a long time, recognized by such visionaries as Simeon the New Theologian (whom we'll be looking at later in this book) and later mystics such Jacob Boehme and, certainly, Thomas Merton. And remember: Sometimes things that don't seem to belong to the theory of prayer are actually there in the practice. The stepping from cataphatic into apophatic perception simply by stilling the faculties is such an innate soul wisdom that it's hard to believe it would remain unknown in a spiritual crucible as intense as that first great desert proving ground.

## The Benedictine Legacy

It is no coincidence, however, that Merton, Keating, and Main, these three great restorers of the Christian heritage of contemplative prayer, are all Benedictine monks. For it is not so much in the distant headwaters of desert spirituality as in the near waters of their own Benedictine spiritual practice that these monks instantly recognized the clear and obvious home of meditation in the Christian West. Its immediate context is in the great Benedictine practice of praying the scripture known as *lectio divina;* and specifically, in the fourth stage of *lectio,* known as *contemplatio,* or contemplation.

Like meditation itself, *lectio divina* is one of those treasures of Christian spirituality that has been in the tradition all along but was virtually unknown outside the monasteries till a generation or so ago. Developing organically out of those early practices of the desert, it offers a simple but comprehensive practice of praying the scripture that leads gradually but steadily from the mind to the heart, and from cataphatic processing modes to apophatic opening. One takes the word of God deeper and deeper into oneself, until finally it returns to the silence which is, as John of the Cross intimated, "God's first language," out of which both Word and words emerge.

This deepening process is approached in four stages. It is customary to think of them as four sequential steps, but this is not necessarily so. While they most often follow sequentially, it is much more helpful to see them as four "stations," like points on a compass, which, after the first, can be connected in any order.

The first station is known as *lectio*, or reading. At this first stage a very short (no more than a few verses) passage of scripture is read, slowly and aloud if at all possible, As this takes place, open yourself deeply to divine guidance and allow yourself to be drawn to the sentence, phrase, or even single word that seems to resonate with a particular kind of vibrancy or attunement. This first and key step in *lectio* is founded on the faith that scripture is a living word—not just the history of an encounter with God that happened long ago, but one that continues to resonate and feed us in our own times.

The second station, typically, is *meditatio*. In this classic Christian usage, the term *meditation* really means a concentrated effort of the faculties. You bring your mind, your feelings, your personal associations, your visualization to bear on the passage to try to get inside it and become intimate with it. If, for example, you've selected for your *lectio* a portion of the parable of the Prodigal Son (Luke 15:11ff.), you might ask yourself which character you're most drawn to, and why; which one most nearly resembles your own basic stance toward life. Or you might puzzle over and even struggle with the generosity of the father, pondering the meaning of his action and whether it challenges your normal sense of fairness. You might notice, in particular, your response to his promise to the older: "My son, you are always with me, and all that I have is yours."

The third station, *oratio*, means "prayer," and it is at this stage that your own deepest feelings are invited into play. Suppose, for example, that you were pondering that sentence "My son, you are always with me and all that I have is yours," and it suddenly struck you forcefully that, through the words of the father in this parable, God is addressing that same reassurance directly to you! Suppose you were to feel the guardedness of your own heart relaxing as the promise that you have always been seen and loved began to reverberate in you. And suppose feelings, even tears, of gratitude began to rise in you as that place deep within was touched. Then you would be having a direct experience of *oratio*, at its fullest. This is the station at which scripture moves down from your head and begins, through your feelings, to engage your heart.

But there is still a fourth station, which is known as *contemplatio*, or "contemplation." As early as the sixth century St. Gregory defined *contemplatio* as "resting in God." At this point in the process all the mental and even emotional work is suspended. The faculties are stilled, and one simply rests in the presence of the divine—"like a weaned child with its mother" in the words of Psalm 131, the monks' favorite metaphor for that stage. After all the cataphatic work, you "stop," either by conscious choice or through a suffusion of divine love (later to be known as "infused grace") that overwhelms the faculties and renders them into stillness.

It is exactly here, at this "still point of the turning world," that the Benedictine monks intuitively recognized the true home of meditation within Christian spiritual tradition, and also its authentic context. Unlike the positioning of meditation in Eastern spiritual traditions, as a spiritual practice in and of itself, in Christianity, Word and silence form a sort of "breathing," which is at the heart of the Christian path to inner awakening. It is not an isolated activity, to be undertaken too far removed from the Word. Rather, this fourth station of *lectio* is what makes it possible for the Word to be fully ingested—to be taken deeper than the levels of ordinary awareness and rational understanding and begin to reverberate in the ground of your being. *Contemplatio* becomes a "womb," in a sense, in which scripture is enfolded in stillness and then reborn, deep within a person's heart, in a quickened conscience and more vibrant archetypal imagination.[15]

When Father William Meninger and the monks at Spencer developed the practice of Centering Prayer, it was with the intuitive recognition that they were neither copying an Eastern method nor grafting a foreign branch onto a tree, but re-creating a precious, even crucial step in the "breathing" of Christian spirituality that in recent centuries had been slowly allowed to wither and die. Described within its classic monastic context, Centering Prayer is a very simple method for bringing people into the fourth station of *lectio*, that place where the faculties are left behind and one simply enters the stillness. Its place in Christianity is authentic, time-tested, and crucially important.

Why had this crucial piece been forgotten? A look at that key question will be the subject of our next chapter.

# 7 ◎ The Loss and Recovery of the Christian Contemplative Tradition

**B**asically, the story of the collective amnesia that fell over Christianity with regard to its own contemplative heritage is probably contained in one simple reality: Our minds like to make ladders. Remember how in the last chapter I urged you to consider the four stages of *lectio divina* as "stations" rather than "stages"? While the distinction may seem like a nuance, there is a strong reason for respecting it: stations suggest a circular movement; ladders lead upward. You climb a ladder in order to get somewhere.

Practically, picturing *lectio* in a circular format—rather like a compass rose, as I suggested in the last chapter—allows for a good deal more fluidity in the process. Depending on your state of being, *lectio* is always a little bit different. Some days the mind will be full and sparkling, and your *meditatio* will be filled with insights. Some days the feelings will be deeply engaged, and you'll find the words of scripture catapulting you into prayer. Other days, for no explicable reason, the feelings just won't come; in this state, you find yourself skipping *oratio* and dropping straight into *contemplatio*. Sometimes, having spent that time in contemplation, you move out of it into an *oratio* that stirs itself to new depths; or an insight that began to incubate in the stillness will lead you back into *meditatio*. It can go in any direction, always simply being attentive to the movements of the spirit.

This freeform, more fluid approach is not spoken of much in the prayer manuals, but it is the way *lectio* actually tends to be practiced by seasoned contemplatives.[1] I was taught it by my hermit teacher at St. Benedict's Monastery in Snowmass, who had been working with *lectio* in this way, about two hours every morning, for more than twenty years. Organically, *lectio* tends to weave as it will, creating ever-unfolding patterns of beauty and insight from the moment-by-moment encounter of divine truth and human receptivity.

In the twelfth century, an Italian Carthusian monk named Guigo II gave *lectio divina* its first official packaging as a "ladder."[2] His influential little book, *The Ladder of Monks* (*Scala Clausatralium*), was not so much an innovation, however, as a skilled reading of the signs of the times, for his fascination with spiritual upward mobility had already pretty well permeated monastic consciousness. As early as the sixth century, the influential Orthodox spiritual master John Climacus (i.e., "John of the Ladder") had introduced the idea of *scala*, or "steps" in prayer, a notion which the equally influential Simeon the New Theologian developed extensively in his tenth- to eleventh-century teachings on the same subject.[3] When applied to *lectio divina*, this schematic created a picture of sequential, upward-leading links. Thus, *lectio* led to *meditatio* led to *oratio* led to *contemplatio*. *Contemplatio* became the highest grade, the pinnacle of the ladder of prayer.

Guigo's ladder came at the headwaters of the era that would see the rise of scholasticism and the loss of the rich, allegorical imagination that had heretofore been the staple of Benedictine visionary experience. Under the sharp edge of the scholastic dissecting scalpel, it did not take too long for these sequential steps of prayer to be further separated out into different *types* of prayer, and finally into types of prayer suitable for certain types of people. More and more the thrust was to see *contemplatio* no longer as the ground of prayer but as its highly rarified apex, best suited to a few rarified types of people known as contemplatives.

Eight centuries later, this was still the spiritual climate solidly in place throughout Catholic Christendom when Thomas Keating began his term as abbot of Spencer in 1961. Outside of the monastery contemplation was something virtually unheard of; in fact, Keating recalls one conversation with a young man studying for the priesthood who, when he asked his seminary professor about contemplative prayer, reportedly received the answer "Oh, that's best left to the boys up there at Spencer!" If those young seekers who had first shown up at the doors of St. Joseph's Abbey in the early 1970s were astounded to discover that Christianity had a contemplative path at its heart, it is at least partially because this had become one of Christianity's best-kept secrets.

Even within the monastery, things were not noticeably better. *Lectio divina* had basically stalled out at the second stage, now known as "discursive meditation," where monks were confined to the very cataphatic practice of meditating (i.e., intellectually and emotionally reflecting on) the Christian Mysteries until engulfed in an overwhelming attraction to contemplative stillness. Even then, permission to follow this attraction was not necessarily or easily granted due to the strong monastic mindset that "infused contemplation," as it was now known (to distinguish it from "acquired contemplation," an outer emulation of the genuine article), was an extremely rare gift, granted only to a precious few. Thomas Keating has spoken sometimes of the rather ticklish catch-22 built into acknowledging a contemplative vocation: since it was officially regarded as the highest and most rarified of vocations, to consider oneself called to it might be seen as a sign of pride—or in other words, a sign that one was not sufficiently "pure in heart" to be entrusted with it.

The very absurdity of this impasse suggests that something is deeply flawed in the basic paradigm of such a spirituality and in this case the flaw is not hard to spot. It is the inevitable consequence of a rupture that should never have been allowed to happen in the first place. As I tried to suggest in the last chapter, in the Christian spiritual path word and silence belong together in an organic and mutually life-giving way, rather like a breathing. The organic, circular process of *lectio divina*, moving from mind to feeling to stillness and back again, becomes the driveshaft of a deeper and much more important transformation: the awakening of what is sometimes called "the eye of the heart," or the ability to understand the words of scripture not only with the mind, but with a deepening interiority that engages both conscience and the visionary imagination. This deepening process is described in monastic tradition under the heading of "the four senses of scripture." Little by little, as the monk perseveres in *lectio*, his understanding progresses through a series of stages: from the literal (preoccupied with linear causality and facts and figures) through two intermediate stages (variously known in the tradition as the moral and allegorical or the Christological and tropological[4]), which develop the powers of the analogical imagination and begin to engage the personal unconscious. The fourth and final stage is known as the anagogical or unitive. At this stage one is fully using those more subtle perceptivities of spiritual awareness—the "spiritual senses," as they're known—to see and taste the presence of the divine as it moves fully in and out of everything. It is not "unitive" simply in the sense of dissolving the multiplicity back into a One, but in the sense of seeing the One beautifully and radiantly illuminating the multiplicity, like light pouring through a stained-glass window, present in both the unity and the diversity. This is the particular genius of the Christian path: the ability to see—really *see*—the particularity and apparent duality of this world not as an illusion, but rather, as a crucible in which the most tender and intimate particularity of the divine heart becomes fully manifest. At the unitive level Christianity is "all heart"—and in this unitive seeing, deeply mystical and poetic, Christianity becomes radiant with the flame of its own innermost truth, like the bush that burns but is not consumed.

When word and silence are separated, the driveshaft grinds to a halt, and this deepening process is suspended. Severed from its nurturing ground in contemplative silence, word tends to become unduly analytical, linear, and dialectical. A vicious circle is set in motion. The farther one strays from the wellsprings of spiritual awareness and the seeing that flows from them, the more one is dependent on the only other processing mode: ordinary awareness and the egoic identity that emerges from it.

And of course, this is the history of Western Christendom in a nutshell. As the age of scholasticism advanced and the Church gradually lost the capacity to read its own mystical roadmaps, both its theology and institutional life grew more dogmatic and contentious. The Protestant Revolution, the Renaissance, and finally the Enlightenment are inevitable steps in a domino chain whose cause lies in the gradual loss of the ability to access, and finally even to believe in, the existence of a selfhood deeper than the selfhood of ordinary awareness, or a wisdom way of knowing that relies on subtle perceptivities invisible to the cataphatic mind.[5] From "blessed are the pure in heart, for they shall see God," the Christian West had become stranded in "I think, therefore I am."

Of course such huge leaps over history leave out significant pieces of the puzzle. In both Catholicism and Protestantism one saw the regular emergence of devotional and mystical movements as Christian seekers intuitively tried to find their way back to the basic contemplative rhythm of word and silence. Quakerism is one such movement, and as I mentioned earlier, it is through Quakerism that I received my own first exposure to contemplative prayer. But if the contemplative reawakening of the late 1960s came as such a "revolution" to those who had grown up in contemporary mainstream Christianity, it is certainly a testament to how far Christian practice itself had drifted from its original moorings.

When Thomas Keating and his brother monks began to introduce Centering Prayer at those pioneering retreats at St. Joseph's Abbey, the practice was initially met with concern from certain bishops and theologians, who were very worried about "bypassing" the three first steps of *lectio* and moving directly into *contemplatio*. There was fear that people would simply turn their backs on the whole cataphatic dimension of scripture and liturgy and lose themselves in apophatic "navel gazing."

Exactly the opposite happened. As a new generation of Christian seekers took eagerly to the waters of Centering Prayer, their "deep immersion" experience of *contemplatio* began to stir a greatly renewed interest in both Bible study and participation in Christian community. *Lectio divina* groups started to spring up everywhere and are still the fastest-growing segment of the Contemplative Outreach's program for contemplative reawakening. In all, it is a quiet but telling confirmation that Guigo's ladder remains, in fact, a circle: word leading deeper into silence; silence breathing new depth and vitality into word.

## Acquired and Infused Contemplation

Before leaving the subject of misconceptions that have greatly crippled the practice of contemplative prayer in the West, I need to say just a bit about this notion of "acquired" versus "infused" contemplation, for it still very much dogs the path of Christian contemplatives. If you embark upon a practice of Centering Prayer, you'll sometimes meet the objection (inevitably raised by clergy person, spiritual director, or others with formal theological training) that contemplation cannot be acquired through spiritual practice; it is given only by God as a gift of "infused grace." It is beyond the reach of all human techniques.

This understanding has so dominated the mindscape of Western spirituality that Thomas Keating himself devotes special attention to it in his teaching on Centering Prayer. Picking his way carefully through the theological minefields, he clarifies that Centering Prayer is not contemplation per se, but only a "method of approaching" contemplative prayer by "removing the obstacles" that stand in its way. His reassurance that such an approach is both possible and fruitful is an important step in the right direction, a confirmation of an innate soul wisdom after centuries of theological nay-saying. But in my opinion, the argument needs to be made even more emphatically; it is time to scrap these categories altogether.

By way of a bit of perspective, the "acquired/infused" issue seems to cause trouble only in the rather narrow swath of religious consciousness, which, for better or worse, is the one most of us happen to inhabit: the Christianity of the West. The term *infused contemplation* first presents itself in the teachings of the sixteenth-century spiritual master John of the Cross, and the distinction between acquired and infused versions of the contemplative state increasingly becomes a preoccupation for those following in John's wake.[6] As far as I am aware, this concern does not seem to factor in any of the other great religious traditions, even in Orthodox Christianity, where it is simply assumed that the work of "bringing the mind down into the heart" is a combined meeting of human effort and divine grace. To put it more succinctly, the yearning to fall to center is itself the result of a force of gravity already drawing us to center, and this gravity is God. "The eye with which you seek God is the eye with which God seeks you," as Meister Eckhart put it. Or as it is beautifully expressed in that Merton quotation we looked at in Chapter 5: "This act of total surrender is not merely a fantastic intellectual and mystical gamble; it is something much more serious. It is an act of love for this unseen person, who, in the very gift of love by which we surrender ourselves to his reality also makes his presence known to us."

The distinction between acquired and infused contemplation makes sense only in the light of that earlier conceptual error—i.e., the portrayal of contemplation as an exalted and rarified state, which as a consequence creates the question "Who is a contemplative?" The real roots of the dilemma lie with Guigo.[7] Establishing the schematic of a ladder with "contemplative" as the top rung inevitably sets in motion a subtle competitiveness: a preoccupation with attaining the highest seat, the "state" of infused contemplation, which more and more comes to be equated with mystical experience rather than unitive seeing (and the two really *are* different!).[8] In other words, the "acquired/infused" checkpoint is really engendered by the egoism that created the problem in the first place; it stipulates that in the final analysis power and control remain with God. This kind of confusion is what ensues when one tries to describe an apophatic process using cataphatic reference points.

What troubles me far more about this whole "acquired/infused" dichotomy, however, is the fact that it rests on a theology of God as "out there," giving graces to some, withholding them from others. This creates much completely unnecessary anguish. "If infused contemplation is the goal, then why do so few people manage to reach it?" asks one recent commentator, who then proceeds to list impediments that might block the onset of the contemplative gifts: everything from personal sin to an overly active temperament, to the fact that God has other plans in mind.[9] Contemplation is viewed as an "add-on," not intrinsic to human nature (though containing its highest fulfillment), but bestowed or denied according to the inscrutable will of God. As they say back in Maine, "You can't get to there from here."

But that God "out there," the God of scholasticism and of a Newtonian universe, is precisely what is countermanded by the contemplative experience itself. I enter the cave of the heart and discover there that God is alive and interpenetrating, in, of, and around, illumining and enflaming all. My own heart is a hologram of the divine triune heart, love in motion, and the finite and infinite realms are connected by an unbreakable bond of mutual yearning. This "in here" vision of God is not only closer to the vision of Jesus and the mystics; it is also increasingly confirmed by the discoveries of contemporary scientific understanding. As the popular Episcopal preacher and theologian Barbara Brown Taylor writes, regarding the radical shift in her image of God brought about by her exposure to quantum physics:

> Where is God in this picture? God is all over the place. God is up there, down here, inside my skin and out. God is the web, the energy, the space, the light—not captured in them, as if any of those concepts were more real than what unites them—but revealed in that singular, vast net of relationships that animates everything there is.[10]

Contemplation, understood in the light of a hologram universe, is not a special gift. It is simply seeing from the perspective of oneness, or in other words, from the level of our spiritual awareness. It can indeed be practiced, and over time, with sincerity and persistence, it becomes an abiding state of consciousness. At times this unitive seeing may sweep you up into rapt adoration; at other times it simply deposits you powerfully and nakedly in the present moment. Either form is an expression of the same underlying consciousness. It is this consciousness itself that is the attained state of contemplation, and it is neither infused nor acquired, because it was never absent—only unrecognized.

# 8 ⑥ The Theology of Centering Prayer

"**B**y their fruits shall you know them. . . ." While the most direct way of making the case for Centering Prayer as an authentically Christian practice is by tracing its roots in Christian scripture and tradition, another approach is to explore its *theological* resonance. In other words, how well does Centering Prayer fit within the core theological reference points of Christianity? On what aspects of Christian self-understanding does it shed light? How does it help one to become a better Christian, to open oneself more deeply to the transformative power of the gospel?

When put to the test of these questions, I believe that Centering Prayer not only holds its own, but in fact *comes into* its own. Perhaps more than any other method of meditation, it proves itself intimately compatible with a foundational Christian self-understanding, illuminating some crucial but subtle theological nuances not easily accessible to the cataphatic mind alone, and in the process validating its own integrity as a method. In fact, as I hope to show later in this chapter, I am increasingly of a mind that it is *only* within the distinct particularities of the Christian theological milieu that Centering Prayer's innovative methodology becomes fully intelligible.

## Dying to Self

The obvious place where meditation—any form of meditation—plugs into the Christian theological mainstream is through the additional light it sheds on Jesus' gospel instructions: "Whoever would save his life will lose it and whoever loses his life will find it" (Matthew 16:25).[1] This is of course a foundational teaching, modeled in Jesus' life even more than in his words, and as Christians we are bound to emulate it. Our life is to be a continuous "dying to self": a voluntary relinquishing of a smaller or more relative life in order to actualize a larger and more permanent one. But what kind of dying is Jesus really talking about here? At what level is this teaching intended to be taken?

In classic Christian moral theology, dying to self is generally interpreted as dying to self-*will*. In other words, we all have our wants, needs, preferences, opinions, and agendas, some of which may be authentic expressions of our being but many of which are motivated (or at least aggravated) by fear and self-importance. Dying to self means being willing to let go of what I want (or think I want) in order to create space for God to direct, lead, and guide me into a truer way of being. This understanding finds its paradigm in Jesus' own struggle in the garden of Gethsemane and his ultimate willing surrender: "Not my will but thine be done, Oh Lord." Whenever there is the appearance of two wills, mine and God's, the smaller will must eventually bring itself into alignment with the larger one so oneness can be restored and the divine truth and mercy can manifest itself in my life. This is certainly an important and valid way of understanding what dying to self is. But is there another way, one that penetrates still deeper into the existential dimension of this teaching?

I remember being struck more than a decade ago by a comment made by Father Laurence Freeman, successor to Dom John Main in the teaching of Christian Meditation, during a homily for All Souls Day at the Benedictine Priory in Montreal. Pondering what meditation has to teach us about Jesus' own death, Father Laurence remarked, "Every time we meditate, we participate in the death of Christ."

He is quite right, of course. The practice of meditation is indeed an authentic experience of dying to self—not at the level of the will, however, but at the level of something even more fundamental: our core sense of identity and the egoic processing methods that keep it in place. When we enter meditation, it is like a "mini-death," at least from the perspective of the ego (which is why it can initially feel so scary). We let go of our self-talk, our interior dialogue, our fears, wants, needs, preferences, daydreams, and fantasies. These all become just "thoughts," and we learn to let them go. We simply entrust ourselves to a deeper aliveness, gently pulling the plug on that tendency of the mind to want to check in with itself all the time. In this sense, meditation is a mini-rehearsal for the hour of our own death, in which the same thing will happen. There comes a moment when the ego is no longer able to hold us together, and our identity is cast to the mercy of Being itself. This is the existential experience of "losing one's life."

I think the inference is obvious: Just as in meditation we participate in the death of Christ, we also participate in his resurrection. At the end of those twenty or so minutes of sitting, when the bell is rung, we are still here! For twenty minutes we have not been holding ourselves in life, and yet life remains. Something has held us and carried us. And this same something, we gradually come to trust, will hold and carry us at the hour of our death. To know this—really *know* this—is the beginning of resurrection life.

This existential understanding of the "losing one's life/finding one's life" paradox is significant in two important ways. First, it allows us to hear Jesus' message of inner awakening within the context of the wider Wisdom tradition to which this teaching actually belongs. As I mentioned earlier, virtually all the great spiritual traditions of the world share the conviction that humanity is the victim of a tragic case of mistaken identity. There is a "self" and a Self, and our fatal mistake lies in confusing the two. The egoic self, or cataphatic self, is in virtually every spiritual tradition immediately dispatched to the realm of the illusory, or at best, transitory. It is the imposter who claims to be the whole. This imposter can become a good servant, but it is a dangerous master. Awakening—which in Jesus' teaching really boils down to the capacity to perceive and act in accordance with the higher laws of the Kingdom of Heaven—is a matter of piercing through the charade of the smaller self to develop a stable connection with the greater Self. In the terms we have been using in this book, this means becoming intimate with our spiritual identity, the sense of selfhood carried in our spiritual awareness. Whenever we make this shift from egoic to spiritual awareness, we are authentically "losing our life"—even if it is only for the duration of the meditation period![2]

Once this existential dimension is seen, it not only reorients the roadmap but also puts in our hands important practical tools for transformation. The role of meditation in service of the gospel becomes much more clear: it creates a bridge between these two levels of awareness within us, offering a consistent and reliable way of practicing the passage from small self to greater Self. When, during the time of meditation, angry or frightened or self-justifying thoughts arise, we use whatever method our practice teaches (saying the mantra, inner witnessing, letting go, etc.) to help us stay clear of attachment (which drags us immediately back to our smaller self) and connected to that deeper level of awareness. With patience and persistence, these skills first patterned in meditation can be transferred to "real life" so that we actually begin to *live* like the Good Samaritan, the woman at the well, or the generous father in the parable of the Prodigal Son. Through meditation it gradually becomes ingrained in us that "losing one's life," regardless of the action that may ultimately be required of us in the outer world, entails first and foremost a passage from our ordinary awareness to our spiritual one, because only at this deeper level of non-fearbased, wholistic perception will we be able to understand what is actually required of us. In fact, more than a few recent writers have suggested that Jesus' well-loved Kingdom of Heaven is none other than this: life lived from the perspective of an attained spiritual awareness.[3]

## Kenosis

So far what I have been saying applies to all meditation, regardless of the method used. But though all paths lead to the same goal—to the direct nurturance of our spiritual awareness—I believe that Centering Prayer comes closer than any other method to fully assimilating the Christian theological and devotional milieu. This is so because its methodology most fully reflects Jesus' own self-understanding and way of going about things. It encapsulates the core gesture of Jesus' life, known from the earliest days of Christian theological reflection as *kenosis*, or self-emptying.

St. Paul sets forth the principle of *kenosis* in his beautiful hymn in Philippians 2: 9–16, prefacing his comments by saying, "Let what was seen in Christ Jesus be seen also in you":

> Though his state was that of God,
> yet he did not claim equality with God
> something he should cling to.

> Rather, he emptied himself,
> and assuming the state of a slave,
> he was born in human likeness.

> He being known as one of us,
> Humbled himself obedient unto death
> Even death on a cross.

> For this God raised him on high
> and bestowed on him the name
> which is above every other name.

> So that at the name of Jesus
> every knee should bend,
> in heaven, on earth and under the earth,

and so every tongue should proclaim
"Jesus Christ is Lord!"
to God the father's Glory.[4]

In this profound theological reflection, Paul sees that self-emptying is the touchstone, the core reality underlying every moment of Jesus' human journey. Self-emptying is what first brings him into human form, and self-emptying is what leads him out, returning him to the realm of dominion and glory. Whether he is moving "down" or "up" the great chain of being, the gesture remains the same.

This passage has been the subject of extensive theological commentary, usually with an eye toward distinguishing two types of love, human and divine: a formula whose most succinct statement belongs to Swedish theologian Anders Nygren: "*Eros* [human love] is man's way to God; *agape* [divine love] is God's way to man."[5] Human love goes up, divine love comes down. Since in every circumstance of his life Jesus practiced this "coming down" kind of love, the theological use usually put to this hymn is as further testimonial to Jesus' divine nature.

But what if these are not two types of love but *two pathways of the same love:* two operational modes within the cosmos with equally legitimate but very different purposes? What if Jesus is not so much revealing his divine nature as leading us along a particular trajectory of divine self-manifestation that has immediate practical consequences for our own *human* journey of self-manifestation? This would be *kenosis* understood from a metaphysical standpoint rather than a theological one, and it is this alternative approach I want to explore here.

For the vast majority of the world's spiritual seekers, it does indeed seem that the way to God is "up." As we saw in the last chapter, the image of the ladder is deeply imprinted in our human spiritual imagination. To ascend is to move closer to God, toward the freedom and luminosity of pure spirit; to descend is to move further away, toward the density and confinement of "flesh." And since to ascend requires energy, in the spiritual realm as well as the physical, the vast majority of the world's spiritual technologies work on some variation of the principle of "conservation of energy." Within each person there is seen to reside a sacred energy of being (sometimes known as the "chi," or life force), which, if not dissipated through the pursuit of bodily pleasures and unconscious psychological agendas, can be conserved and concentrated to provide the additional energy required for transformation. Through the disciplines of prayer, meditation, fasting, and inner witnessing the seeker learns how to purify and concentrate this inner reserve and how to avoid squandering it in physical or emotional lust, petty reactions, and ego-gratification.[6] This universal strategy, which Nygren terms *eros* but I like to think of more informally as the "store-it-up" school, is at the basis of all genuine asceticism (i.e., asceticism understood as a method of transformation, not self-mortification), including our own Christian asceticism. And there is a good reason for this: The strategy works. As self-mastery is attained through physical and moral purification, the spiritual energy concentrated within a person becomes strong enough and clear enough to sustain contact with increasingly higher and more intense frequencies of the divine life, converging at last upon the unitive point.

There is another route to the center however: a more reckless and extravagant path, which is not through storing up the energy, but through throwing it all away—or giving it all away. The unitive point is approached not through the concentration of being, but through the free squandering of it. This paradigm, which I like to think of as the "throw-it-away" school, works on the principle that the energy of being is infinite and flows to us from an unstinting Source if we can merely allow this flow to happen. In Christianity, this understanding is expressed through the path of *kenosis*.

If the goal of concentrative spiritual practices is union, *kenosis* seems to have a particular affinity with new manifestation. Self-emptying is also, in the deepest sense, *self-disclosure*, which is fundamentally a creative act; it tends to bring new worlds into existence by revealing what had formerly been present only in potential. From a metaphysical perspective, explosion rather than implosion is the principle of actualization. Many of the most subtle Christian theologians believe that this is how God originally created the world, through a radical self-outpouring: "the prodigal who squanders himself," as Karl Rahner puts it.[7] It is also, clearly, how Christ redeemed it—storing up nothing, clinging to nothing, equally at home in humiliation and glory. His ultimate act of self-emptying upon the cross is what brings into being the New Creation—i.e., the Kingdom of Heaven made fully manifest.

The most sublime descriptions of this alternative path are undoubtedly to be found in the Sufi mystic Rumi, whose verses below are a worthy companion piece to Paul's great hymn:

> Love is recklessness, not reason.
> Reason seeks a profit,
> Love comes on strong, consuming herself,
>     Unabashed.
>
> Yet in the midst of suffering
> Love proceeds like a millstone,
> Hard-surfaced and straight-forward.
>
> Having died to self-interest,
> She risks everything and asks for nothing.
> Love gambles away every gift God bestows.[8]

We can see how this poem precisely describes the trajectory that Jesus followed. His idea of "dying to self" was not through inner renunciation and guarding the purity of his being, but through radically squandering everything he had and was. In life he horrified the prim and proper by dining with tax collectors and prostitutes, by telling parables about extravagant generosity, by giving his approval to acts of costly and apparently pointless sacrifice such as the woman who broke open the alabaster jar to anoint him with precious oil; by teaching always and everywhere, "Lay not up for yourselves treasures on earth." John's disciples disapproved of him for drinking and banqueting; the Pharisees disapproved of him for healing on the sabbath. But he went his way, giving himself fully into life and death, losing himself, squandering himself, "gambling away every gift God bestows." It is not asceticism but *tantra*—love utterly poured out, "consum'd with that which it was nourish'd by," in the words of Shakespeare's sonnet[9]—that opens the gate to the Kingdom of Heaven. This is what Jesus taught and this is what he walked.

And he left us a method for practicing this path ourselves, the method he himself modeled to perfection in the garden of Gethsemane. When surrounded by fear, contradiction, betrayal; when the "fight or flight" alarm bells are going off in your head and everything inside you wants to brace and defend itself, the infallible way to extricate yourself and reclaim your home in that sheltering kingdom is simply to freely release whatever you are holding onto—including, if it comes to this, life itself. The method of full, voluntary self-donation reconnects you instantly to the wellspring; in fact, it *is* the wellspring. The most daring gamble of Jesus' trajectory of pure love may just be to show us that self-emptying is not the *means* to something else; the act is itself the full expression of its meaning and instantly brings into being "a new creation": the integral wholeness of Love manifested in the particularity of a human heart.

As Paul so profoundly realized, "up" and "down" do not ultimately matter, for in *kenosis* consciousness reclaims dominion over energy. The pathway to freedom, to the realized unity of our being, lies in *and in fact is coextensive with* the sacramental act of giving it all away, making "self-giving" the core gesture through which all the meaning, purpose, and nobility of our human life is ultimately conveyed.

## Centering Prayer and Kenosis

What does this have to do with Centering Prayer? Plenty. Of all the methods of meditation, it most purely approximates meditational *kenosis*. It is pure self-emptying.

The vast majority of other meditation methods are built on the model of "storing" or "attaining": One "concentrates" so as to attain clear mind, conscious presence, a strong witnessing "I," or unitive experience. Thus, there is a subtle dissonance between the goal of self-emptying and the means used to attain it.

But in Centering Prayer, one aims to attain nothing: not clear mind, steady-state consciousness, or unitive seeing. It is a prayer that simply exercises the kenotic path: love made full in the act of giving itself away. It is practice, over and over, with that one bare gesture.

Apart from this grounding in *kenosis*, the practice of Centering Prayer may not fully make sense. Later on in this book, we will look, in fact, at criticism sometimes leveled at Centering Prayer by those used to more concentrative methods, questioning the advisability of letting go of everything, including the "I am" presence and the mantra. But when this instruction is understood not as the deliberate cultivation of an interior vacuum ("sinking mind," as it's sometimes called), but rather, as a willing divestment of all possessions even up to and including personal consciousness, its appropriateness becomes clear—and its ability to inform the Christian life dazzling. Slowly, steadily, Centering Prayer patterns into its practitioners what I would call the quintessential Jesus response: the meeting of any and all life situations (including the final one, where a concentrative method is no longer possible) by the complete, free giving of oneself. So understood, its compatibility with Christianity is not only clear, but inescapable.

# PART III

## The Psychology of Centering Prayer

# 9 ⑥ The Divine Therapy

**W**hen Thomas Keating and his confreres at St. Joseph's Abbey first began developing Centering Prayer in the late 1960s, they were thinking entirely in terms of a renewal of contemplative prayer: the creation of an indigenously Christian form of meditation in response to the massive defection of younger Catholics to Eastern spiritual paths. Based largely on the fourteenth-century *Cloud of Unknowing*, Centering Prayer took its place among other Christian meditational forms sprouting up at the time, particularly Christian Zen prayer, and the "Christian Meditation" of Dom John Main. It was a devotional method pure and simple, a way of deepening and intensifying the relationship with God. There was at that point no psychological underpinning attached to it, nor even a clue that one might exist.

Then in the summer of 1983, Keating organized the first Centering Prayer Intensive at the Lama Foundation in San Cristobal, New Mexico, hoping to achieve a more concentrated meditative experience on the model of a Zen *sesshin*, or "deep immersion" retreat. It lasted a full two weeks, and its effects were impressive—and a bit unsettling. While Keating and several others in the group were well experienced in deep meditation, no one was prepared for the volume and vibrancy of emotional outpouring that flooded forth from five hours a day of Centering Prayer practice. Tears, repressed memories, deep intuitions all jumbled to the surface—along with a sense of catharsis and bonding among those dozen charter participants, remains substantially unchanged to this day. From his years as abbot, Keating was used to the gradual sensitizing and participation of the unconscious during the course of contemplative life—but not with such speed and intensity. He recalls seeing "people going through in ten days what it would have taken them twenty years to go through at a monastery." What had happened? He quickly realized he had a tiger by the tail, and his suspicion was that it lay in the methodology of the prayer itself.

As we saw earlier in this book, Centering Prayer is a surrender method, or, to describe this same motion from a psychological rather than a theological standpoint, a *receptive* method. It does not entail a concentration but rather a *relaxation* of attention so that there is no longer a single-pointed focus for the mind. Transpersonal Psychology was at that point still in its infancy, but it has since confirmed what Keating discovered through direct observation: the more receptive the meditation method, the greater and more immediate the involvement of the unconscious. Concentrative methods, which always entail a certain degree of egoic effort, tend to retard the participation of the unconscious. Receptive methods, on the other hand, foster it, particularly in an intensive group situation such as that pioneering Lama retreat.

But Keating's real intuitive leap was to recognize the import of this observation: this "unloading of the unconscious" as he would later call it, was not an inconsequential side effect, but a significant *purification* process at work. In fact, this was the connecting link he had long been looking for, between purification as traditionally presented in Christian teaching (as a reprogramming of conscious motivation, or the struggle against sin), and the realization from contemporary psychology that such reprogramming

92

goes only skin-deep, and in fact can cause serious damage if used for repression and denial of unconscious impulses. "The real ascesis is the purification of *unconscious* motives," Keating had long argued—but how to get at them? With Centering Prayer as a catalyst for the unconscious, he found his tool—and his paradigm.

Thus Centering Prayer was reborn not merely as a devotional method but as a psychological one as well. In the decade following that first Lama retreat, recognizing the need to provide support and a conceptual framework for the growing ranks of Centering Prayer practitioners, Keating produced first a 24-tape video series, then a series of books—*Open Mind, Open Heart* (1986), *The Mystery of Christ* (1987), *Invitation to Love* (1992), and *Intimacy with God* (1994)—in which he unfolded an increasingly cohesive and subtle vision of the Christian "spiritual journey": the path of inner healing and transformation that begins when one embraces a regular practice of Centering Prayer.[1]

Today it is for this teaching that he is primarily known and upon which his enormous popularity as a spiritual teacher rests. In his words, "The Method of Centering Prayer was specifically developed as a dialogue between contemporary psychological models and the classic language of the Christian spiritual path."[2] That "classic language," which envisions a progression through purgative, illuminative, and unitive stages, has guided the journey of many a saint, but for many reasons both good and bad often fails to resonate with the spirit of contemporary times, where "woundedness—recovery—wellness" comprises the prevailing paradigm for transformation. In an ambitious and innovative synthesis, Keating interweaves the traditional wisdom of Thomas Aquinas, Teresa of Avila, and John of the Cross with the contemporary insights of Ken Wilber, Michael Washburn, Jean Piaget, and even the Twelve Step Method of Alcoholics Anonymous. The result is a comprehensive psycho-spiritual paradigm that begins in woundedness and ends, if a person is willing to take it that far, in transforming union. He calls it the Divine Therapy.

In this chapter I wish to present the major contours of this system as simply and impartially as I can. I don't claim to "buy" the whole teaching uncritically. It has a few significant holes, both theologically and therapeutically, and in the next chapter I will offer some reservations and points that seem in need of further refinement. But overall, his synthesis is both sound and timely, and its influence on the contemporary spiritual scene has been enormous. Anyone who seriously takes up the practice of Centering Prayer needs to be familiar with this teaching in preparation for some familiar tight spots along the path. And even for those who do not personally practice this prayer, it's still important to know one's way around the basic concepts and nomenclature simply because of the powerful sway these concepts now hold in the fields of contemporary spiritual psychology and spiritual direction.

## Apophatic Psychotherapy

Keating's teaching begins by a fundamental repositioning of the place of meditation in a spiritual praxis. Rather than seeing it as a tool for developing concentration, relaxing stress, or accessing higher states of consciousness, he sees it primarily as a catalyst for the purification and healing of the unconscious. This purification is itself prayer—not a preparation for relationship with the higher, but the relationship itself. It is the essence of what he means by "consenting to the presence and action of God."

How does this purification work? As the unconscious unloads during Centering Prayer, these small purifications are actually a part of a larger project. One begins to dismantle the "false self," i.e., the needy, driven, unrecognized motivations that govern most of our untransformed human behavior.

Dovetailing classic Christian teaching and contemporary psychology, Keating suggests the false self as a modern equivalent for the traditional concept of the consequences of original sin. Beginning in infancy (or even before) each of us, in response to perceived threats to our well-being, develops a false self: a set of protective behaviors driven at root by a sense of need and lack. The essence of the false self is driven, addictive energy, consisting of tremendous emotional investment in compensatory "emotional programs for happiness," as Keating calls them.

It is the false self that we bring to the spiritual journey; our "true self" lies buried beneath the accretions and defenses. In all of us there is a huge amount of healing that has to take place before our deep and authentic quest for union with God—which requires tremendous courage and inner presence to sustain—escapes the gravitational pull of our psychological woundedness and self-justification. This, in essence, constitutes the spiritual journey.

So far this is orthodox psychological and theological fare. But where Thomas Keating takes the bold step is by his assertion that Centering Prayer is a direct catalyst to this process of purification of the false self. As one sits in centering prayer with the intent to rest in and trust in God, the unconscious begins to unload "the emotional junk of a lifetime." Repressed memories, pain, accumulated dull hurt rise to the surface and are, through the attitude of gentle consent, allowed to depart. As Keating visualizes the process in *Invitation to Love:*

> The level of deep rest accessed during the prayer period loosens up the hardpan around the emotional weeds stored in the unconscious, of which the body seems to be the warehouse. The psyche begins to evacuate spontaneously the undigested emotional material of a lifetime, opening up new space for self-knowledge, freedom of choice, and the discovery of the divine presence within. As a consequence, a growing trust in God, a bonding with the Divine Therapist, enables us to endure the process.[3]

"Thus," he continues, "the gift of contemplative prayer is a practical and essential tool for confronting the heart of the Christian ascesis—namely, the struggle with our unconscious motivation—while at the same time establishing the climate and necessary dispositions for a relationship with God and leading, if we persevere, to divine union." As I see it, the most fruitful connection here is his interlinking of the "dark night" or "cloud of unknowing" of the traditional apophatic path with the psychological process—the "dark" of the "ground" or of our psyche. If psychoanalysis might represent "cataphatic therapy"—that is, using words, concepts, awareness to illuminate the darkness of our inner ground, so Centering Prayer is in fact being presented as a kind of "apophatic psychotherapy." What really happens when one enters the cloud of unknowing, resting in God beyond thoughts, words, and feelings, is a profound healing of the emotional wounds of a lifetime. As these wounds are gradually surfaced and *released* in prayer (one simply lets them go non-possessively, rather than retaining them for inspection as in psychoanalysis), more and more the false self weakens and the true self gradually emerges. For Keating this is the real meaning of the term *transforming union*. As he states quite plainly in *Intimacy with God:* "We can bring the false self to liturgy and to the reception of the sacraments, but we cannot bring the false self forever to contemplative prayer because it is the nature of contemplative prayer to dissolve it."[4]

Keating does not claim that such a practice replaces the need for cataphatic psychotherapy. Indeed, material that arises out of the unconscious in prayer sometimes requires the assistance of psychotherapy; this is particularly true in cases of retrieved memories of emotional or sexual abuse. But in Centering Prayer this healing and purification occur within the sanctuary of prayer, combined with a deepening trust in God. So at the same time that healing is going on at the psychological level, a deepening of the spiritual faculties is occurring as well—recollection, vigilance, attention of the heart—leading to a blossoming of the traditional theological virtues of faith, hope, and love.

## The Shape of the Journey

As was discussed extensively in the preceding chapter, we are used to thinking of spiritual transformation as an *ascent*. The effects of a spiritual practice, we expect, are to make us calmer, more able to cope, more filled with equanimity.

The Divine Therapy model, however, suggests a different scenario: that the ascent is inextricably bound to a descent into the ground of our own psyche (this would be the principle of *kenosis* viewed from a psychological standpoint). Thus, periods of psychological ferment and destabilization are signs that the journey is progressing, not that it is a failure. As a practice of meditational prayer loosens repressed material in the unconscious, the initial fruits of spiritual practice may not be the expected peace and enlightenment, but destabilization and the emergence into consciousness of considerable pain.

One woman in our group in Maine experienced this process particularly vividly. After only a few weeks of regular practice of Centering Prayer, she found herself increasingly tense and irritable, and frequently went home from meditation to pick a fight with her husband. She was tempted to quit, but with the encouragement of the group she stayed on and cooperated with the process.

What was happening (rather quickly in her case) was that a brittle control—keeping everything at a superficial level of "niceness"—collapsed almost immediately in the face of her immersion in contemplative silence. She found herself face to face with a deep guilt about what was in fact her second marriage and a terror that God would punish her and her husband with cancer. Needless to say, "resting" in such a God was not a tranquil experience! But with a good deal of courage she has been able to face these feelings, work through them, and re-establish a relationship with both her husband and God on a deeper, freer level.

In my own practice of this prayer, I have learned by repeated experience that the "reward" for a period of committed sitting is often the emergence of a patch of pain long buried and several days of emotional turmoil. Keating calls it "the archeological dig." As trust grows in God and practice becomes more stable, we penetrate deeper and deeper down to the bedrock of pain, the origin of our personal false self. The results are often personally horrifying, but again, says Keating, this does not mean that the spiritual journey is a failure, but that it is doing its job.

The fruits of this unloading are more than worth the pain. In response to each significant descent into the ground of our woundedness, there is a parallel ascent in the form of inner freedom, the experience of the fruits of the spirit, and beatitude.

There are several practical implications to this, but the paramount one—for both spiritual seekers and spiritual guides—is to recognize that Centering Prayer is a psychological method and will produce results in that realm, some of them initially painful. In *Intimacy with God* Keating recounts how a graduate student recently did a thesis on Centering Prayer, along with several forms of Eastern meditation, recommending them as a way to reduce anxiety. Keating wrote back to the man saying, "Centering Prayer will reduce anxiety for perhaps the first three months. But once the unconscious starts to unload, it will give you more anxiety than you ever had in your life." For individual practitioners he recommends a limited dosage—twenty to thirty minutes twice a day is the normal prescription—to prevent the premature emergence of material into the conscious. Ten-day retreats rely on a trained staff to help handle a more intensive unloading process. But Keating insists that the method is safe, and that only in the case of serious depression or psychotic symptoms should the prayer be disallowed or discontinued.

## From Healing to Holiness

While there are gaps in Keating's model, far more important are the gaps that are being bridged: between theory and practice, and between contemporary psychology and the traditional language of spiritual purification. By repositioning meditation as a tool for the purification of the unconscious—and insisting that people *do* it, not just talk about it—he can be faithful to contemporary models of healing and wholeness while pointing the way beyond, toward profound transformation in ever-deepening surrender. In so doing, he has rescued us both from the vagueness of contemporary psycho-jargon, and from the violence of traditional metaphors, based on renunciation, vigilance, and "spiritual warfare" (as if a part of us had to be killed, or at least thoroughly locked up, in order for holiness to grow).

In the "Divine Therapy" spiritual transformation is gentle, and it always holds paramount the need for integration of psyche and spirit. The one cannot dominate the other; they must proceed apace. If the spirit's role is to be strong, the psyche's is to be vulnerable, and the lion must lie down with the lamb before the peaceable kingdom will reign within. Throughout the entire teaching, the touchstones are gentleness, patience, consent, and a willingness to let the process of integration unfold with its own pace and authenticity. Of course there is woundedness, but there is holiness as well. How the two come together—not which one wins, but how they join—constitutes the unique and profound meaning of one's life: the emergence out of the maelstrom of the true self, transformed in Christ.

# 10 ⑥ From Healing to Holiness

Every metaphor both illumines and veils its subject, and the metaphor of the "divine therapist" is no exception. On the plus side, it offers an enormously accessible starting point for the recovery-minded temperament of our times. It fits hand-in-glove with the basic thrust of the Twelve Step Program of AA and other popular recovery programs, for which it serves as a natural extension, and it has recently been gaining attention for its phenomenally successful prison ministry.[1] Anyone who has ever struggled with an addiction—or even the fiercely compulsive quality of the false self programs—will recognize the immediate practical relevance of God seen as "divine therapist."

But the metaphor has its drawbacks as well, and if taken too literally or pushed too far, it can wind up distorting the very path it is trying to illuminate. In this chapter I'd like to look at a few of these potentially negative side effects and suggest places where temperance may be in order in the use of this metaphor.

Of course, the first distortion comes from forgetting that the "divine therapist" is a metaphor in the first place, not a literal paradigm. "God is *like* a divine therapist," is what Thomas Keating intends; he's speaking in the language of poetry, not of science. But metaphor is always a somewhat risky business; once you leave that "like" out, there are always some who will hear the analogy as literal truth. Given Keating's enormous stature as a spiritual teacher there is sometimes a tendency among his followers to pass on his teachings as gospel truth, without sufficient appreciation of either the poetry or humor nuancing his delivery. Precisely because his teaching is so influential, it's important to be aware of the places where the divine therapy metaphor can get off track or create unintentional distortions. From my experience with this teaching, there are three potential sand traps that need to be carefully avoided.

## Healing the Ego or Transcending It?

Classic psychotherapy takes place within the domain of egoic functioning; its goal is to improve it. Through therapy, wounded and dysfunctional people get the help they need to live better-adjusted and more successful lives. Weak and damaged egos gain self-esteem, and overly defended ones learn to relax and enjoy the ride.

Classic spiritual work, no matter what the religious tradition, is about transcending the ego. It seeks to awaken within a person something that is recognized as "true self," or higher Self. This does not necessarily mean eliminating the ego, but rather displacing it as the seat of one's personal identity. The process is rather like discovering that the earth revolves around the sun rather than vice versa.

Now in Keating's version of the journey, the problem is that these two very different objectives start out looking like dead ringers for each other. When one sets out on this journey to "dismantle the false self," exactly what is it that is being dismantled? And when it has been dismantled, who or what is the self that remains?

The term *false self* does not originate with Thomas Keating; you'll find it extensively in the writings of Thomas Merton and a number of other spiritual writers. But it is nearly always used in a generic sense, more or less synonymous with egoic functioning itself. For Merton the ego is *per se* the false self: the part that mistakes itself for the whole and creates its own reality in ignorance of (or defiance of) its connection to divine being.

In adapting the term to his own teaching, Thomas Keating adds a very significant nuance. In his version, the false self is always wounded; it comes into being specifically as a defense mechanism against perceived threats and deprivations during infancy and early childhood (and even in the womb). Drawing heavily on modern developmental psychology, he traces how the false self arises out of what he calls "the energy centers": woundings in the three core areas of security/survival, esteem/affection, and power/control. These woundings in turn set in motion a vortex of attractions (things a person requires in his/her life in order to feel safe and affirmed) and aversions (things that "push his/her buttons"). The false self is by definition neurotic, and it is at least theoretically a preventable mistake since its roots ultimately lie in inadequacies of nurturance (whether intentional or unintentional). Keating's false self is not just egoic functioning per se, but a particularly maladapted egoic function in need of proper diagnosis and treatment.

This more restricted use of the term dovetails nicely with classic developmental psychology. But it inadvertently introduces another possibility into the equation. If the false self is defined as a distorted manifestation of egoic being, then the all-too-obvious inference is that the true self would be the ego healed of its distortions and defenses, or in other words, the healthy ego.

When and if this mistake is made, ego transcendence drops out of the picture, and "the divine therapy" becomes just plain old therapy. Transcendent selfhood winds up with nothing to clearly distinguish it from simply high egoic functioning; or in other words, the ability to makes one's way successfully in the world without the continuous negative drag of the false self programs. In and of itself, there is no harm in high egoic functioning, of course. But the danger lies in confusing the sense of "wellness" that comes from relief of neurotic symptoms—and the ego still solidly in its comfort zone—with the "grace beyond grace" that comes from genuine ego transcendence.[2]

Thomas Keating himself is profoundly aware of the difference between these two states, of course, and if you read carefully between the lines, you'll see that his teachings on the "fruits of the spirit" and "contemplative gifts of the spirit" that emerge as part and parcel of the purification process are his way of alluding to the second, or ego-transcending, process going on in the midst of the therapeutic work.[3] But the subtlety of this distinction is not always caught and not always carefully enough sustained in the teaching itself. From his presentation of the "archeological dig," for example, which I mentioned in the last chapter, it is easy to get the impression that the "healing of the emotional wounds of a lifetime" will eventually, *in and of itself*, lead to transforming union—or in other words, that the therapeutic journey somehow spontaneously evolves into ego transcendence. Exactly how this evolution takes place, or what distinguishes deep healing at the psychological level from true unitive consciousness, is not made sufficiently clear.

Given this gray area in the teaching it seems best simply to reiterate the traditional understanding in schools of inner work. While healing is an important aspect of the journey toward holiness, the healthy ego must never be mistaken for the true self. It does not somehow evolve into the true self.[4] Whether healthy or unhealthy, the ego is still the ego and as such is still inescapably tied to the domain of the lower, or provisional, selfhood. In the classic language of the Christian spiritual path, it cannot exceed the "illuminative" stage because it is trapped within the experience/experiencer dualism by virtue of its basic operating system: the self-reflexive "I" that sees the world through the subject/object polarity.[5]

Whatever "true self" may look like when described theologically, *operationally* it involves the shift to a different kind of consciousness (called non-dual or "unitive" in classic Christian terminology), which flows out from that deeper place within us, described earlier as our "apophatic awareness." Inner evolution almost always begins through an awakening of the connection with that deeper, more unboundaried consciousness within us—as in Centering Prayer, of course. But once this has been experienced, the shift of gravitation from egoic to transcendent or "true" self has traditionally been carried out in inner work through the development of a stable "witnessing" presence or inner observer, whose purpose is to keep track of the larger picture and mediate between these two legitimate but very different senses of selfhood. (I will be discussing this practice in more detail in Chapter 12.) Without this mediating presence, even the healing that comes from deep purification and surrender won't spontaneously transmute into unitive consciousness.

For our immediate purposes, however, the main point is to keep in mind as you work with the metaphor of the divine therapy that the goal of this "therapy" extends far, far beyond therapy as traditionally constituted. It's really about sanctification. It's the "therapy" of the Mystery of Christ.

## "For God so loved the world . . ."

You enter therapy because something's wrong with you, right? Either you've become aware that some aspect of your personality is constantly tripping you up, or else life itself has become so unmanageable that you simply have to take yourself in hand. Modern psychotherapy (which, incidentally, has only been around for a bit more than a century) has its roots in gross pathology; its founding father, Sigmund Freud, formulated his theories through dealing with patients who were basically psychotic. As a healing profession, psychotherapy's primary concern is with the movement from disease to wellness, from severe dysfunction to successful adaptation.

Built right into the therapeutic metaphor, then, is the tendency to want to regard the false self system as a disease, a pathology that needs curing. And since we all seem to be born with false self systems, it's understandable how one might begin picturing the human condition as itself a disease: pathology "writ large."

This is a mistake we simply can't afford to make. It's one of those places I alluded to at the beginning of the chapter where if we start to let the metaphor run away with us, it winds up in serious distortion.

Granted, it's easy to fall into the trap. Christian theology still tends to view the fall of Adam as a *mistake*, the spoiling of a plan that was intended to come out otherwise. Through the teachings of Augustine on original sin and the dark Jansenism that has brooded over so much of Western Christendom,[6] it's all too easy to slip into thinking that there is indeed something irreducibly, incorrigibly wrong with us human beings and that "recovery" is about the best we can manage.

But what about Genesis 1:31: "And God saw all that he had made, and it was good"? Or John 3:16: "For God so loved the world that he gave his only Son"? Certainly violence and darkness seem to be the common lot of untransformed humanity, but these dark elements are counterbalanced by astonishing acts of compassion, forbearance, and creativity that are equally part and parcel of our human sphere. The light and darkness exist within a dynamic continuum whose focal point seems to be human consciousness.

Moreover, the relationship between light and dark may be far less obvious than a simple medical model would suggest. ("Darkness is a pathology; cure it.") What if the apparent ubiquity of the false self system had another explanation, other than sin and pathology? What if—as poets and mystics have long intuited—the reservoir of human darkness is not so much a disease as the raw material of our transformation; or in other words, without the false self system as the precondition of our humanity, there would be no journey and no transformation?

This seems to be the view both of classic schools of inner awakening, and, if I read them correctly, of modern Jungian and Transpersonal Psychology. True self comes into being as a kind of sacred alchemy, through the conscious acceptance and integration of our shadow side. It is not so much the curing of a pathology as the birthing of something that would never have existed apart from struggle, like a candle that reveals its true nature only when tallow and wick are set aflame.

I saw this alternative model powerfully at work in my teacher Raphael, the hermit monk of Snowmass. He carried deep wounds from a painful and even tragic childhood. But his yearning for complete unification in Christ was so powerful that it propelled him along the path, far more powerfully than if his inner psychological world had been more comfortable. Toward the end of his life, his biggest surprise was not that he had transcended his humanity, but that he could finally accept it! Again, we need to remember that ego-healing and ego-transcendence happen simultaneously not sequentially along the path of our lives, and that our wounds, entrusted to the divine mercy, can become the stimulus to extraordinary growth.

No matter how in tune with the recovery-minded temperament of our times, the divine therapy as metaphor needs to keep its feet firmly planted in the strong Biblical conviction that creation is good, and that the Fall, while it may have tarnished the *likeness* of God in the human person (i.e., the fully realized manifestation of the Divine Indwelling), in no way destroyed the image, the Divine Indwelling itself. "The glory of God is a human being fully alive," said Bishop Irenaeus in the third century, in words whose bold invitation we still shy away from. The human condition exists for a purpose far more majestic and compelling than simply getting well.

## Getting Off the Couch

"Regression in the service of ego-transcendence" is a phrase drawn from the contemporary psychotherapist Michael Washburn.[7] The idea is that people undergoing therapy need to be given a safe space where it's okay to "regress"—in other words, to become completely vulnerable to their unconscious and the shadow material it holds.

This is the third area in which I would urge some caution against allowing the therapeutic metaphor to get out of hand.

The idea of ego-regression, in its aspect of sacred vulnerability, corresponds closely with what Keating sees as the heart of the divine therapy. As we enter the "safe space" of Centering Prayer, trusting in the divine therapist, our egoic defense mechanisms loosen their grip and the "emotional wounds of a lifetime" are able to come to the surface and be spontaneously evacuated.

Given this dovetailing, it's not surprising how deeply the basic metaphor of the psychotherapist's couch has imprinted itself on both the nomenclature and the basic operational style of Contemplative Outreach. Centering Prayer meetings are called "support groups" (rather than "prayer groups" or "meditation groups," two other obvious possibilities),[8] and the structure of the popular ten-day intensive retreats in many respects paraphrases the model of deep psychotherapy. (Many people come to these retreats expecting an intense uncovering process, to be accompanied with manifest tears and inner vulnerability. The job of the staff is to provide a safe space for this apophatic primal therapy to happen.)

The down side, however, is that participants can become so focused on their personal healing and the safe space needed to facilitate this that they can forget that Centering Prayer is first and foremost *prayer:* on behalf of the world and in solidarity with all other human beings.

The most striking display of this forgetfulness I have ever seen occurred at a Centering Prayer retreat at Snowmass more than a decade ago. Keating himself was leading our meeting, a small gathering of advanced practitioners of the prayer for what he was in those days calling his "issues workshops." We had all been watching a video together, and as it ended, Father Thomas, hauling his six-foot-plus frame rather too quickly off the couch, twisted his ankle and came crashing to the floor.

That launched what would turn out to be several very difficult years in his life. The shock from that fall set off a domino chain of ailments, which finally settled in as severe chronic fatigue syndrome.

The incident occurred right at the end of our workshop, and we carried on with out final meeting and then the obligatory group closure. As we went around the room sharing what the week had been like for us, nearly everyone had been deeply shaken by Father Thomas's accident. But one man, a Protestant minister, verbalized his upset in no uncertain terms. "I have to admit, I'm very, very angry," he began. "I work extremely hard all year long being there for others. I'd been counting on this week as a safe space to do my own work. Father Thomas's fall took away my safe space."

Admittedly, this is an extreme example, and in no way characteristic of the generosity and goodness that have overwhelmingly characterized more than twenty years of intensive Centering Prayer retreats. But the incident has stayed in my memory because it does point to a danger inherent in the therapeutic metaphor itself: that under the guise of "vulnerability" and "transference to the divine therapist," people are simply permitted to linger in self-absorption, far beyond what is healthful either for themselves or for the community of which they are a part.

Centering prayer teaches from the outset that the fruits of the prayer are to be found in daily life, and this is an important touchstone to keep coming back to. The "therapy" does not happen just on the "couch"—i.e., in the sanctuary of the prayer period itself, or in the "safe space" of a retreat format; the real crucible of transformation occurs when prayer encounters daily life. Unlike the "regression" of psychotherapy, the "surrender" of Centering Prayer is an active exercise of spiritual strength and mutuality, and these qualities are immediately available to us, *even in the heat of the unloading process*, to meet life's changing circumstances with flexibility and compassion. We need to keep remembering that. My concern is that the therapy metaphor, taken too literally, may cause people to underestimate the reservoir of strength and divine assistance available to them at any moment through the sheer fact that Centering Prayer is indeed *prayer* and not therapy.

At any rate, it is important for Centering Prayer groups to keep reminding themselves that they are first and foremost Christian communities, and that the current psychotherapeutic preoccupation with "closed groups" and "safe spaces" must always give way before the basic Christian imperative to hospitality and compassionate service. Contemplative prayer is first and foremost an act of worship: an offering of the prayer of self-disclosure and inner surrender on behalf of the world, not as a group therapy session by "clients" whose goal is personal healing.

# PART IV

## Centering Prayer and Inner Awakening

# 11 ⑥ Attention of the Heart

$A$sk most people what meditation is, and they're likely to respond that it is about stilling or collecting the mind. Our usual jumbled, self-referential, reactive thinking is no more capable or mirroring reality than a storm-tossed lake is capable of mirroring the clear image of the moon. First you have to still the waters, slow down those wild leaps of the monkey mind. Once the mind is calm and concentrated, it becomes better able to access those deep states of peacefulness and unitive seeing that lie beneath our ordinary awareness.

"Clear mind," then, is the usual goal of meditation, at least in the vast majority of the world's meditation methods. Rather than allowing oneself to become lost and dissipated in the individual contents of consciousness, one learns through meditation how to hold the mind in a kind of doubled attention that is simultaneously present both to the contents of consciousness and the field itself.

Perhaps less obvious is the fact that a state of presence requires a "someone" who is present. This is generally known as the "witnessing presence" or "observing I," and the creation of this stable inner viewing platform is also a standard goal of traditional meditation practice. One learns how to move from the tunnel vision of ordinary awareness to the larger and more spacious presence that resonates with one's spiritual awareness. The usual methodology for making this shift lies in harnessing the mind's capacity to pay attention. Whether by watching the mental phenomena as they come up (as in awareness methods), or by honing the mind to a simple task like saying the mantra or following one's breath (as in concentrative methods), the idea is that the act of sustaining attention from that place of inner, conscious presence gradually liberates the mind from its servitude to the smaller, egoic self and allows it to become more and more the still reflecting mirror of Divine Presence itself.

Centering Prayer teaching also seems to acknowledge to this witnessing presence—or so it first appears. In Thomas Keating's popular metaphor of the boats on the river, which we encountered in Chapter 4, he likens the position of the meditator during prayer time to a scuba diver sitting on a rock at the bottom of the riverbed. Thoughts float by like boats on the surface of this river of consciousness, but the diver simply continues to perch there on his or her rock, allowing the thoughts to pass by overhead. The description sounds very close to a classic witnessing presence in awareness meditation, and on this basis Centering Prayer has often been classified as an awareness practice.

But there is one very significant difference. In classic awareness meditation, the watcher would stay keenly tuned to the passing parade overhead, watching each boat as it emerged into view, sent its wake rippling through the waters, and then passed out of sight. But in Centering Prayer the diver simply wakes up to discover that somehow he's managed to sleepwalk into the hold of one of those boats; at which point he simply climbs off and swims back down to his rock. There is no requirement for sustained observing consciousness, merely for prompt action when one discovers oneself "caught out."

Because in most schools meditation is seen as virtually synonymous with clarity of mind and a strong "I am here" presence, it is to the considerable horror of some practitioners on these more traditional paths that Centering Prayer seems to go sailing right by these core prerequisites for either single-pointed attention or a sustained witnessing presence. Christian Meditation's founding father, John Main, echoes the traditional wisdom when he insists that it is absolutely essential to keep saying the mantra as a touchstone for attention. To fail to do so, he says, leads to a state that he calls "pernicious peace."[1] In attempting to describe this state, he, too, is drawn to the metaphor of boats on a river. As he sees it, meditation is something like rowing a boat across a river; the goal is to get to the other side. Partway across the river, the midday sun may feel warm and gentle, and the temptation is strong to simply pull in the oars and bask in the sun. While the consequent experience is pleasurable, the net result is that you simply float downstream. Getting to the other side requires that you keep pulling steadily on the oar, which for Main means the steady repetition of the mantra.

What is this "other side" that the meditator is so determined to reach? Presumably it is the state of "clear mind" that concentrative and awareness practices set such a high store on. From the perspective of Christian meditation and most other traditional practices, the instruction in Centering Prayer not to say the Sacred Word consistently—but only when you notice you're engaged with a thought—seems to invite a moving away from the duties and discipline of conscious presence into a dreamy, hazy state that may be pleasurable, but in which a good deal of time is wasted in simple vapidity. Drowsy, perhaps delightful, but one does not make it to the other side of the river.

In fact, according to some meditation teachers, Centering Prayer not only allows but deliberately cultivates a state known in Buddhist tradition as "sinking mind"—defined by one teacher as "when there are no thoughts but there is nobody present."[2] In other words, it's a deliberate cultivation of emptiness. The inner landscape can be quiet and thought-free, but without that connection to a conscious "I am" presence, time is merely wasted.

These reservations from experienced practitioners of more traditional paths are significant enough to deserve a careful response. From the perspective of concentrative and awareness practice, Centering Prayer looks like sleeping at the post, not paying attention. But is there more than one way to pay attention? I believe there is, and that the key to understanding Centering Prayer's unique integrity and effectiveness as a path lies in recognizing this.

It is true that Centering Prayer is a "drowsier" form of meditation than is generally typical. It seems to work in a band much more akin to REM sleep; in fact, practitioners do occasionally fall asleep, a strict "no-no" in more traditional forms of meditation.[3] We have seen already how Thomas Keating turns Centering Prayer's natural interface with the unconscious to good advantage in his concept of the "purification of the unconscious," the cornerstone of his divine therapy paradigm.

But in addition to its obvious affinity with the unconscious, is there something more going on in Centering Prayer than meets the eye, a way of being present that is sustained through a whole different mechanism of self-awareness? I believe this is the case. There is an attention of the mind, which does indeed entail single-pointed concentration and a conscious presence. But there is another way of paying attention that makes its way along a very different pathway of knowing: different, but no less effective. It is called attention of the heart.

## Attention of the Heart

The term *attention of the heart* comes from Simeon the New Theologian, a Greek Orthodox spiritual master of the late tenth century. His curiously little-known essay "Three Forms of Attention and Prayer" is one of the most important resources available for locating Centering Prayer within the wider tradition of Christian interior prayer and for validating its innovative yet entirely orthodox starting points.[4]

Simeon was one of the most brilliant spiritual theologians of his day, or of any day. His lifespan (949–1022) places him almost exactly a thousand years ago, but the issues he was grappling with are still cutting edge in our own times. Essentially, Simeon insisted on the dimension of conscious presence in our human relationship with the divine. This landed him on the wrong side in many a theological dispute—as for example, when he argued that the quality of attention of the priest affects the validity of the mass: a position that is theologically untenable (it appears to make divine grace dependent on human action), but certainly experientially valid. It's obvious to nearly everyone that a mass rattled off by rote by a priest doing six of them in one day, while it may remain theologically valid, is missing an essential element. Presence, or as Simeon calls it, "attention of the heart," is the capacity to be fully engaged at every level of one's being: alive and simultaneously present to both God and the situation at hand.

Developing attention of the heart is all-important, Simeon maintains, because without it, it is impossible to acquire sufficient inner strength to fulfill the beatitudes.[5] To translate his insight into the terminology we have been using in this book, Simeon clearly sees that ordinary awareness *per se* is incapable of carrying out the gospel. Only when the mind is "in the heart," grounded and tethered in that deeper wellspring of spiritual awareness, is it possible to live the teachings of Jesus without hypocrisy or burnout. The gospel requires a radical openness and compassion that are beyond the capacity of the anxious, fear-ridden ego.

But how to swim down to these deeper waters? Simeon lays out three routes toward the goal of "putting the mind in the heart." The first is through the concentration of affectivity, which I described earlier as the traditional route in both the Christian East and Christian West for making the passage from the cataphatic to the apophatic. Following this method, a person "imagines celestial blessings, hierarchies of angels and dwellings of saints . . . [ponders] all he has learned from Holy Scriptures, gazing up to heaven and thus inciting his soul to longing and love of God, at times even shedding tears and weeping."[6]

This is essentially the charismatic prayer of our Western tradition, or, in *lectio divina*, the delicate movement from *meditatio* to *oratio*. The problem, Simeon asserts, is that it relies on a high level of excitement of the external faculties, which is ultimately self-delusional and can become addictive, leading one to depend on lights, sweet scents, and "other like phenomena" as evidence of the presence of God. "If then such a man give himself up to silence," Simeon adds bluntly, "he can scarcely avoid going out of his mind."[7]

The second methodology is self-examination and the collecting of thoughts "so that they cease to wander"—the classic methodology of a practice based on attention and conscious awareness. But the fatal flaw in this methodology, he observes, is that such a practitioner "remains in the head, whereas evil thoughts are generated in the heart."[8] In other words, the aspiring seeker is likely to be blindsided by the strength of his unconscious impulses, and the deeply imprinted response pattern of seeking refuge in the watcher, or "observing I," runs the risk of dissociation—"making a religion of one's better moments," to use Jacob Needleman's mordant phrase.[9] If such a practitioner further compounds the problem by vainglory—the conviction that he is the master of his own household—"the unhappy man works in vain and will lose his reward forever."[10]

Simeon designates the third method as *attention of the heart* and describes it as follows:

> You should observe three things before all else: freedom from all cares, not only cares about bad and vain but even about good things. . . . Your conscience should be clear so that it denounces you in nothing, and you should have a complete absence of passionate attachment, so that your thought inclines to nothing worldly.[11]

You can see that Simeon has essentially just described the practice of surrender. That greatest *desideratum* of the spiritual life, attention of the heart, is achieved, he feels, not so much by concentration of either the emotions or the mind as by the simple release of all that one is clinging to, the good things as well as the bad things.

While Simeon is clearly describing an integrated practice combining both prayer and daily life, it is uncanny how closely his words dovetail with the basic methodology of Centering Prayer. As a person sits in Centering Prayer attempting to "resist no thought, retain no thought, react to no thought," he or she is actually progressing in small (but utterly real) increments toward "freedom from all cares" and "the absence of passionate attachments." In fact, the case can be made that what Thomas Keating has really succeeded in doing is to give meditational form to Simeon's attention of the heart, thereby providing a powerful new access point to the traditional wisdom of the Christian inner path. Meanwhile, Simeon's essay is another link in the chain situating Centering Prayer firmly within the lineage of Christian *kenosis* understood as spiritual path.

## "The nothingness of all that is not God"

Simeon's essay, then, gives us a way to begin to make sense of a meditation practice that does not first entail a concentration of the mind. There are different ways of paying attention, he recognizes, each one appropriate to the specific method of prayer or meditation a person is working with and the overall aim of that method. Or in other words, to borrow a line from the poet Philip Booth, "How you get there is where you'll arrive."[12] Transposing Simeon's "three forms of attention and prayer" to the three basic categories of meditation practice we have been discussing in this book yields the following brief schematic:

Concentrative and awareness practices aim at *clarity of mind*. They get there by way of concentrated attention and conscious presence.

Surrender methods arrive at *purity of heart*. They get there by way of relinquishing the passions and relaxing the will.

In a nutshell, the difference between attention of the mind and attention of the heart is that attention of the mind requires a touchstone in conscious presence. That is why these practices hold so fiercely to the mantra or "alert awareness" (depending on the method), and why within the terms of these methods the relaxing of one's grip on conscious presence is experienced as "sinking mind": the descent into a warm, fuzzy unconsciousness.

But Centering Prayer is a surrender practice, and within the terms of this method even that fierce grip on conscious presence becomes merely another thing one is clinging to. It, too, is gently let go, as one simply entrusts oneself to the deeper level, which is not really "unconsciousness" at all, but rather divine consciousness resonating in the heart as "the hidden ground of love," unmediated by a witnessing presence.

Thomas Merton vividly describes this state in a letter to an Islamic friend, Abdul Aziz, written in 1964:

> My prayer tends very much toward what you call *fana* [annihilation in God]. There is in my heart this great thirst to recognize totally the nothingness of all that is not God. My prayer is then a kind of praise rising up out of the center of Nothing and Silence. If I am still present "myself," this I recognize as an obstacle about which I can do nothing unless He Himself removes the obstacle. If He wills, He can make the Nothingness into a total clarity. If He does not will, then the Nothingness seems itself to be an object and remains an obstacle. Such is my ordinary way of prayer, or meditation. It is not "thinking about" anything, but a direct seeking of the Face of the Invisible, which cannot be found unless we become lost in Him who is invisible.[13]

Admittedly, Merton's experience of prayer at these depths pushes the envelope of what most of us would expect or even desire from a meditation practice. It corresponds most closely with what Sufi mysticism would call "prayer of the spirit" (the final step beyond the "prayer of the secret" we looked at earlier) in which, as one writer explains it, "the *spirit* within the one who is remembering—that counterpart within man of the Divine Spirit—contemplates God in *total cognitive silence*."[14] But it is important to remember that even within our Christian tradition this state is well known; a steady stream of witnesses from *The Cloud of Unknowing* to Thomas Merton insist that even personal presence can and must ultimately be transcended in the gesture of surrendering all back into God. Centering Prayer is a first step in the direction of that "ultimate apophatic," and it is within this context that its aim and effectiveness must ultimately be judged—not against the backdrop of "clear mind," which belongs to a different paradigm.

## Magnetic Center

If attention of the heart really exists as a distinct energy (not just a metaphor), where is it carried in the body? The experience of "clear mind" is distinct and breathtaking, like coming up out of a cloud deck. Is there a parallel sensate awareness that accompanies this other form of attention? I believe that there is. It lies in the phenomenon of the "magnetization of the heart."

Throughout this book I have returned again and again to the theme of Centering Prayer as a gesture of self-emptying. So what happens when we actually make that gesture? Is it symbolic only, an underlying attitude, or is there an actual physiological component to it?

When I have raised this question with experienced Centering Prayer practitioners, the answer is a resounding "yes," and there is surprising agreement as to what this physiological component consists of. Virtually all practitioners notice that when they let go of a thought, there is an inner release that is simultaneously a "drop"—from the head or chest to the solar plexus region—followed by a "lift," almost like an in-breath. It is a subtle but distinct kind of inner breathing.

Earlier on in this book I described Centering Prayer as a totally "win-win" situation. Whatever happens to you during the prayer time is just fine. If there are few thoughts and you plunge immediately into a deep stillness, then your prayer that day is an immersion in blessedness. If the thoughts come as insistently as mosquitoes buzzing around your head and you're still doing the best you can to let go, then great! You are getting a good aerobic workout of your "muscle" of consent.

I wasn't being entirely facetious here; in fact, I wasn't being facetious at all. I was referring specifically to this "inner breathing" just described. Every time you are willing to release a thought, to perform the gesture of self-emptying, this gesture is patterned and strengthened within you. In time, with patience and persistence, it begins to take shape as a magnetic center within you, a deeper pull or gravitation that is clearly perceptible, like a tug to center.[15]

There comes a point on the learning curve of Centering Prayer—and it is a very important milestone in the "progress" of this prayer—when you will find yourself attracted to a thought but immediately and willingly let it go because you instantly recognize that the thought will pull you back up to the surface, to a vibration that is less intense and less real than what you are presently engaged with. Your emerging magnetic center is increasingly recognized as the actual inner pulsation of a mutual yearning, yours for God and God's for you. The center begins to quicken, to take on a life of its own.

Not long afterward, you may begin to sense that center calling you even when you are not officially at prayer. In the midst of daily life, even as you move about in your ordinary awareness, you will notice the pulse of that underlying mutual yearning honing you to center. It is like a child you are carrying within you. Even as you go about your daily activities, you can sense it as a deeper life tugging and fluttering within you, reminding you of the greater life to which you belong. Centering Prayer is well named in this respect, because its most powerful physiological effect is that it will tend to develop in you a kind of habitual gravitation from within that is constantly calling you to your depths. In a surrender practice, this is how attention of the heart becomes physically embodied.

Thomas Merton once remarked: "The real freedom is to be able to come and go from that center and to do without anything that is not immediately connected to that center."[16] For in point of fact, magnetic center will carry you home. It is indeed your interior compass, the needle of your heart pointing to the magnetic north of God. When the inner alignment is strong and steady, you find that you are able to follow the course of your own authentic unfolding with a kind of effortless grace. When the signal gets dim or you forget to listen, it's a pretty safe bet that you've wandered off-course.

Even more pertinent from the standpoint of inner work, it is from and through the sensed reality of magnetic center that you will be able to orient yourself as you take on the next and in some ways the most bedeviling challenge of intermediate-level spiritual work: the development and correct placement of the inner "watcher," or witnessing presence. We will turn to this challenge in our next chapter.

# 12 ⑥ Working with an Inner Observer

In classic spiritual training, authentic "work on self" begins with the development of a strong inner observer or witness. "You can't move a plank you're standing on!" was the adage in the inner work group in which I participated. As long as ordinary awareness is the only awareness you know, there is really no possibility of shifting the weight of your being from its egoic orbit to true center. The most you can hope for is a "healthy ego": reasonably in touch with its own boundaries and respectful of the boundaries of others.

In fact, one modern spiritual teacher, Eckhart Tolle, succinctly defines the ego as "the unobserved mind."[1] What makes the ego the ego, he feels, is *precisely* its incapacity to separate from itself, its tendency to get completely lost in its inner psychodramas. Following the traditional language of inner work, he equates this level of consciousness with *un*consciousness, or waking sleep:

> As you probably know, in sleep you constantly move between the phases of dreamless sleep and the dream state. Similarly, in wakefulness most people only shift between ordinary unconsciousness and deep unconsciousness.

125

What I call ordinary unconsciousness means being identified with your thought processes and emotions, your reactions, desires, and aversions. It is most people's normal
state. In that state you are run by the egoic mind, and you
are unaware of Being.[2]

Most spiritual teachers link the inner observer with a state
they call *presence*, or in other words, an active awareness of Being
itself. Rather than getting lost in the contents of consciousness
(those "reactions, desires, and aversions" Tolle speaks of), you
learn to pay attention to the *field* of consciousness as well—not just
the boats floating down the river, but the river itself. Out of this
simultaneous awareness, a whole new sense of "I" emerges: no
longer identified with each passing impulse or emotional reaction,
but deeply planted in Being itself. The inner observer carries this
new sense of "I" and is thus the bridge between egoic awareness
and deeper Selfhood.

## Centering Prayer and the Inner Observer

In traditional spiritual teaching, meditation is the place to begin
to develop an inner observer; in fact, this is usually seen as one of
meditation's primary purposes. Centering Prayer is the exception to
this rule, as we saw in the last chapter. But it is important for Centering Prayer practitioners to realize that this exception is not a permanent waiver. If anything, it's exactly the opposite: *Because* during the
prayer time itself Centering Prayer moves straight to that "ultimate
apophatic," it is even more important for a practitioner on this path
to work diligently outside of the prayer time to develop a conscious
witnessing presence. In fact, this is probably the only way to graduate from what Thomas Keating himself sometimes calls the "K
through 3" version of Centering Prayer—the heavily psychologized
"elementary school" version of the spiritual journey presented in
the "divine therapy" paradigm—into true inner work. It is a huge
growing edge for maturing Centering Prayer practitioners.

Working with an inner observer—getting the knack for this
kind of "doubled awareness," as it's sometimes called—is never

easy and almost always involves a period of acute self-consciousness and wobbling, like learning to ride a bicycle. Our complete identification with our ordinary awareness is so automatic that learning to step back from it, to be in one's life from that deeper place of spiritual awareness, almost always feels stilted and unspontaneous at first. And indeed, getting the hang of this *is* one of the more subtle skills in spiritual work, and there are more than a few ways to go off-course and even do yourself mental damage. Ideally, it is one of those skills best learned hands-on, not from a book. But the problem is that within the mainstream Christian path there are still very few teachers actually teaching it.

In this chapter, then, I would like to offer some basic guidelines and orientation points about working with an inner observer to help you get up and running in the practice. Once a few common misconceptions have been cleared up, the practice is not all *that* arcane, and as I alluded at the end of the last chapter, a foundation in Centering Prayer is actually tremendously advantageous in cutting through some of the more notorious tight spots on the learning curve. In this chapter we'll be concerned with general ground rules, then in the next we'll draw on these as we take a deeper look at the "Welcoming Practice," Centering Prayer's most powerful tool for carrying contemplative prayer into daily life.

## What Is It?

First and foremost, your inner observer is not the interiorized voice of your superego, nor is it your higher egoic self psychoanalyzing your false self. If the word *should* appears anywhere in your messages, you've got the superego instead. It is not the voice of judgment in you, and it has absolutely nothing to do with correct action. It is not self-awareness in the usual sense—that is, you can speak very articulately about whatever issues, feelings, and emotions are coming up for you. Rather, it is Self-awareness, in the sense of shifting your center of gravity from its usual egoic orbit to a deeper place, which essentially watches *through* you, from the perspective of Being itself.

The distinctive feature of the inner observer is that it is *non-identified;* it can watch what is going on without grabbing on to the contents or claiming the process for itself. In ordinary psychological terms, to be self-aware means to be able to say, for example, "I am very angry at you," or "I am feeling sad right now." There is articulateness, but no separation; you are still completely identified with whatever it is you are feeling, and your goal is to get to the bottom of the problem and if possible, to correct it. In inner work, by contrast, the goal is to gain some space between that feeling and that deeper sense of your own selfhood. Students are sometimes taught to say "*It* is very angry" or "*It* is feeling sad" in order to pattern in the realization that *it* is not you; you as consciousness are far deeper and more stable than the passing riot of moods, feelings, and agendas.

The classic name for this state in spiritual work is "doubled awareness," which means the capacity to be simultaneously present, without prejudice, to both the contents of consciousness and the field itself.

In Centering Prayer, of course, you have already been practicing this drill in its apophatic version. As you work with the instruction, "Whenever a thought comes up, let it go," you begin to discover that you in fact *do* have the capacity to separate; when a thought comes up, you can "just say no." Obviously, then, you are not just your thoughts; that mysterious "chooser" in you must emerge from a much deeper and steadier will at the center of your being. Work with an inner observer simply extends this core insight into daily life.

## Where Is It Carried?

The real answer to the question of "what" lies in the question "where." In traditional spiritual practice the inner observer is carried in the mind, and doubled awareness is essentially brought about by dividing the attention—not allowing it to be entirely absorbed in whatever external task or internal emotion is preoccupying it, but holding a part of it always in reserve to pay attention to

Being itself. This is seen as one of the primary goals of the training offered by followers of the Russian mystic G. I. Gurdjieff; when I participated in this training, a good deal of time was spent in deliberate multi-tasking that vastly increased the capacity and flexibility of the mind: counting backward in complicated number patterns while doing simple manual tasks like chopping carrots while sensing our left foot, all the while remembering our deepest yearning.

But in point of fact, the inner observer is not carried in the mind. It is not one part of the mind observing another, and it is not the conscious mind being conscious of itself—at least not at the outset, or in the way you might expect.

This common but serious mistake can lead to the one very real danger in inner observer work, so I will issue the warning here: *Do not, under any circumstances, attempt to observe the observer!* If you do, you will be plunged into a surrealistic hall of mirrors (who is the observer observing the observer observing the observer? etc.). Even for normal consciousness, this will definitely create vertigo; for those less stable it can lead to temporary schizophrenia.

The other risk in attempting to hold the inner observer in your mind is that it can too easily lead to dissociation. Simeon the New Theologian was on to this problem, as we saw in the last chapter, when he pointed out that such a person "remains in the head, whereas evil thoughts are generated in the heart." It is all too easy to use the "ivory tower" of the inner observer, perched at the top of one's head, to go out of contact with the messier and darker feelings swirling up from one's unconscious. Unfortunately, feelings unacknowledged do not go away; they just go deeper.

This is where the "attention of the heart" learned in Centering Prayer is so profoundly helpful. Along this heart pathway, doubled awareness is not a matter of division, but a kind of multiplication, a simultaneity. The inner observer is not carried in the conscious mind being conscious of itself, but lower in your being, in magnetic center. "It" watches through you—that mysterious inner assistance we have spoken about earlier, that seems to be the percolation of that deeper watcher (the Spirit within you) through the deeper unconscious. You do not "do" anything; you merely align yourself with magnetic center, which becomes the vessel of the witnessing presence. Simply move yourself down, physically, in your being and take a couple of deep breaths as you coincide with that tug-to-center already patterned into you.

"Look, Ma, no hands!" Since you are not holding back or reserving attention to attend to consciousness, your mind is entirely free to be present to whatever is at hand. You can give yourself to the situation without worrying about reserving attention for God, self-remembrance, or the inner observer. Somehow all these things are taken care of. "I sleep, but my heart is awake," in the words of the Song of Songs. It is a much more visceral way of being in touch with that deeper yearning within you: not so much a matter of your carrying it as of allowing it to carry you. Once you've gotten the hang of it, this whole business of doubled awareness proceeds far more naturally.

## What Is It For?

Once you've learned where to place your inner observer, you automatically discover what its real purpose is. It's there *to connect the two worlds in you.* It is not, as frequently assumed, a way of bailing out of your small self into your larger self, escaping the horizontal axis of your being in favor of the vertical. Rather, it lives at the intersection of the two axes, and its purpose is to bring them into meaningful alignment. As I said earlier, its job is to be simultaneously present, *without prejudice,* to both the contents of consciousness and the field itself.

This is in itself an important corrective to our usual notion of what spiritual awakening is all about. It is commonly thought that the goal is to override or destroy the lower, or egoic, self and replace it with the higher self. But this is really not what is intended. What is intended is a *marriage* of the two, so that the lower with its essential uniqueness and the higher with its transpersonal brilliance come together as a true individuality. The witnessing presence looks compassionately in both directions, allowing us to see the whole picture and *be* the whole picture.

Because of its primary function as connection, then, the witness is not about dissociation. It is not about "making a religion out of one's better moments," using the higher self to suppress the lower self. In fact, as virtually all genuine spiritual teachers insist, its real function is to bring you into a state of presence, to back you down out of your mind into a full embodiment of your being, so you can feel that the "I am" that courses through God and Jesus is coursing through you as well.

Even more strongly, its purpose is to bring you into a state of *unconditional* presence, so that you not only believe but know that no physical or emotional state has the power to knock you out of presence. It is not a matter of replacing negative emotions with positive emotions—only of realizing that through magnetic center, presence can be sustained regardless of whatever inner or outer storms may assail you. You do not have to make the terror or anger or grief go away; you simply have to hunker down in magnetic center and allow the surface of life to be as it is. Amazingly, you discover that at the depths Being still holds firm.

From an inner work perspective, this is the state Paul is describing when he writes (Romans 8: 38–39): "For I am convinced that neither death nor life, neither angels nor demons, neither the present nor the future, nor any powers, neither height nor depth, nor anything else in all creation, will be able to separate us from the love of God that is in Christ Jesus our Lord." His conviction is certainly true. But it can only be held through an inner observer firmly rooted in magnetic center; it is simply too scary for the mind alone.

## The Power to See

The most important thing to keep reminding yourself about the inner observer is that it is not judgmental and heavy, but essentially playful. It is the quintessential experimenter, always finding new ways to connect the two worlds in you. If, for example, you habitually head to the front of every line, one day you might suddenly find yourself asking, "I wonder what would happen if I intentionally went to the rear?" Or if a person has just pushed your buttons and your blood is boiling, it may suddenly occur to you, "What would happen if I didn't react in the usual way?" "What if?" is its home turf. It likes to stir up the waters of consciousness, win more and more of you away from conditioned reactions and the usual self-justifications into the adventure of Being itself. From the standpoint of the inner observer, life is a vast realm of consciousness to be explored and fulfilled, and its real job is to keep you on your toes.

It seems logical to expect that an increase in seeing should result in an immediate increase in capacity for doing, but this is usually not the case. With practice you may be able to notice when your buttons are being pushed or you find yourself slipping into self-pity or self-righteousness, but noticing it doesn't necessarily make the mood shift. Sometimes the very best you can do is to stay present to what you're seeing, including enduring the gap in yourself between seeing and being able to do. To try to shift into "fix-it" mode will throw you out of your inner observer and back into your superego.

But no conscious seeing is ever wasted. If all you can do is wave goodbye to yourself as you go over the waterfall, this is a billion times more important than changing anything. Seeing creates a new relationship with yourself, and eventually that new relationship will bear fruit in the power to do. But doing is never the point. Every seeing, no matter how calamitous to the ego, is an enhancement of Being, a strengthening of the connection of the worlds within you.

If these points are kept in mind, you will begin to develop a whole new way of living within yourself, and your life will change. This change—and the promise in which it is secured—is beautifully expressed in the final lines of a poem by René Daumal:

> Sometimes a man humbles himself in his heart, submits the visible to the power to see, and seeks to return to his source. He seeks, he finds, and he returns to his source.[3]

"Submit the visible to the power to see": That is the theory and practice of inner observation in a nutshell. The observing "I," carried in magnetic center, becomes the integral point of your being, and around this center intentional and conscious true self begins to manifest.

# 13 ⑥ The Welcoming Prayer

When students of Centering Prayer have progressed through the introductory workshops and intensive retreats and present themselves to become teachers of the practice themselves, one of the most useful pieces of information made available to them during those training sessions is a diagram called "The False Self In Action." Thomas Keating likes to refer to it as "refrigerator art"—i.e., "If you paste this up on your refrigerator, you'll be able to see at a glance what's wrong with you!" Wisecracks aside, it is a wonderfully insightful little piece of analysis about why life lived out of ordinary awareness has the distinct impression of being a vicious circle.

It also beautifully sets the stage for our consideration of the Welcoming Practice, Centering Prayer's powerful companion piece for turning daily life into a virtually limitless field for inner awakening. To get oriented on the diagram, start by noticing the line dividing the page horizontally. Below the line (the part shaded gray) represents the unconscious; above is our so-called conscious state.

In the lower section (1), firmly embedded in the unconscious

135

# The False Self in Action
Emotional programs for happiness based on
institutional needs from early childhood

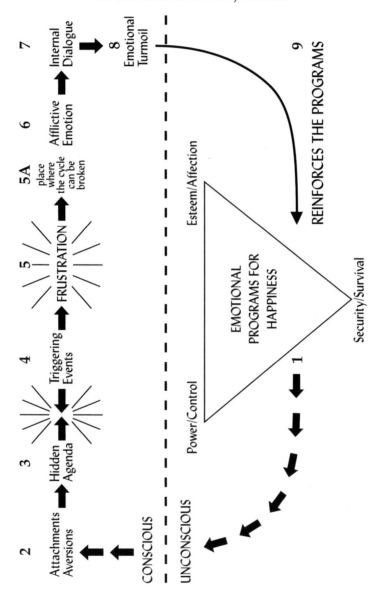

and looking like the Bermuda Triangle it actually is, you'll find those three "energy centers" (as Keating calls them), or in other words, the classic "emotional programs for happiness" of security/survival; esteem/affection; power/control, which comprise the basic building blocks of the false self system. (Refer back to Chapter 9 if you need to refresh yourself on this teaching.) They are called "energy centers" because unconsciously a huge amount of our psychic energy is bound up in identification with these programs.

These unconscious programs percolate into consciousness in the form of attachments and aversions (2). Attachments are things you need to feel safe and comfortable (and these can be ideas and values as much as or even more than physical objects); aversions are those things that "push your buttons." If, for example, you have a major identification with a power/control program, the thought of setting off on a car trip without your motel reservations all lined up might make you very anxious; it would be an "aversion." If security/survival was a huge issue for you, you might be very attached to a regular paycheck or a good retirement plan—so much so that working freelance would be too scary even to consider. These attachments and aversions, semi-conscious and mostly cloaked in self-justification, virtually guarantee that we will enter situations in life with "hidden values," or as they're called on the diagram, hidden agendas (3). You may *think* you're joining the altar guild because you want to serve your church, but underneath, and largely unbeknownst to you, you may have a self-esteem program running: wanting to be appreciated and seen as a "good" person. Or perhaps a power/control program: to be in charge of an important committee and make sure things are done properly.

From this point on, the circle begins to run its inevitable course. "The problem with a power/control program is that you're only in competition with about two or three million other people in the world," Keating comments with his trademark sly twinkle. There seems to be a karmic law that hidden agendas will attract their corresponding "triggering event" or "troubling situation"

(4). If you've taken on that altar guild job, for example, with the hidden agenda of being seen as an important person in the church, you can virtually guarantee that someone else on the committee will be running that same program and you'll find yourselves on a collision course.

At this next stage on the diagram (5), frustration starts to set in, usually obliquely at first. Perhaps you'll be aware of a mounting sense of irritation as you watch this person cutting you off in discussions or making a successful play for the sympathy of other committee members. Perhaps you'll hear her voice get more high-pitched and insistent—yours as well. Perhaps there will be that telltale tightening of your jaw or a knot in your stomach.

At this point, what happens next is usually automatic. That flickering sense of irritation will soon fill in as full-blown emotion as you recognize, "I'm very angry!" At this point of "afflictive emotions" (6) you are fully identified with the feeling of anger and your defenses are swiftly building. Almost immediately thereafter, you will begin to hear the "commentaries" go off in your mind (7). Keating calls these the "pre-recorded tapes"; they are the stories and self-talk we've all programmed into ourselves to meet life's reversals with our own unique brew of self-pity and self-justification. "How *dare* she!" "Every time I try to help out, this *always* happens!" "No one appreciates me." "How can a person like that call herself a Christian?" "My mother always told me I couldn't get along with others," and so on.

The combination of feeling and commentary is like gasoline poured on fire; it keeps the flames leaping higher and higher. Before long this full rolling boil of emotion begins to have its effect on your body (8). You may find yourself with a splitting headache or a churning stomach. It may take hours or even days for you to settle down. Carried in your bloodstream and your muscle tension, this frustration goes back down into the unconscious (9), where it merely reinforces the false self programs that gave rise to it in the first place (1). The next time you stick your nose out and volunteer for committee work (if you ever do again), you are likely to be even more defended, even more desperately identified with your hidden agendas—and hence, even more likely to attract the same frustrating result.

Welcome to the Ferris wheel of the false self system! This little diagram is essentially a full-blown enactment of what Eckhart Tolle means by "ordinary unconscious" and suggests one of the major lines of demarcation separating our usual cultural sense of ourselves from the far less sanguine picture presented in inner work. In classic theological language we like to think of human beings as having "free will"—the ability to make conscious choices. But according to the picture presented in the diagram, human beings in the grip of their false self programs are totally and predictably mechanical. In my own inner work group, one of the adages describing this predicament was called The Typewriter and the Bicycle: "Said the typewriter to the bicycle, 'Why do you keep going around in circles?' Said the bicycle to the typewriter, 'Why do you keep clacking on?'" The point, obviously, is that both of them were machines, only doing what they were programmed to do. Is it really so different with us?

Inner awakening is basically about breaking this cycle, opening to a new infusion of self-restraint or awakened consciousness that knocks you loose from the downed electric wire of that crazy, volatile, emotional energy. It's about being able to make a separation, stepping back into a more spacious inner place so that the whole pattern doesn't just keep playing itself out mindlessly, stealing your vital life energy that can really be used for far better purposes.

So where does Centering Prayer come into all this? Notice on the chart there's a place **5A** (which I skipped over earlier), called "place where the cycle can be broken." It occurs during the nanosecond between that first gathering sense of "frustration" and the moment you actually put the full weight of your being into your frustration, or become "identified," in the classic spiritual language.

This tiny "window of opportunity" has been known and commented on in Christian tradition since at least the fourth century. Evagrius, one of the great desert fathers (sometimes called

Christianity's first spiritual psychologist), recognized there was a brief sliver of time before "thoughts" (*logismoi*, as he called them—the first awareness of inner discomfort) turned into "passions," full-fledged identified emotions. If one could be alert to that moment, it would be possible to avoid getting trapped. Rather than becoming tightly bound up in the feeling of "I," the emotional energy would simply dissipate, and the person could avoid a useless trip over the waterfall.

During the prayer period itself, Centering Prayer is constantly working that edge, that window of opportunity. If a thought comes up—say you're sitting there in the prayer and remember that stormy clash you just had with your boss, and say this "attractive" thought starts to hook you and the emotions start building—you simply apply the guideline: "If a thought comes up, just let it go and return ever so gently to the Sacred Word." Viewed from this perspective, the "letting go" practiced over and over in Centering Prayer is really a letting go of identification, a releasing of a "thought" before it becomes a "passion." And with time and patience, you begin to become adept at this practice.

The next step is simply to learn to do this drill when the boss is actually there right in your face . . .

## Carrying Prayer into Daily Life

The Welcoming Prayer is Centering Prayer's tool *par excellence* for making the transition from surrender understood simply as a methodology of meditation into surrender as an underlying attitude and practice for meeting daily life. Since its development in the 1980s as an active complement to Centering Prayer, this practice has been offered regularly as part of formation training for prospective facilitators and presenters of Centering Prayer, as well as in special workshops.[1]

The Welcoming Prayer is generally taught within a psychotherapeutic context —i.e., as a tool to extend the "divine therapy" into daily life and to gain relief from the afflictive emotions of the false self system. And it is indeed a very effective way of nipping false self programs in the bud and restoring inner calm.

But it is even more powerful as a tool of inner awakening: for strengthening the observer "I" and "submitting the visible to the power to see," and when used in this fashion, is one of the strongest practices I have ever encountered for a rapid increase in both the quality and quantity of awakened consciousness. It's from this perspective that I want to consider it here.

The founding genius behind the Welcoming Prayer was a woman named Mary Mrozowski, who from 1983, when she showed up at that fateful first Lama Foundation retreat, until her death in 1993 was one of Thomas Keating's closest associates and a prime mover in the development and popularization of his teachings. For those privileged to know Mary, the practice is immediately recognizable as a direct reflection of her vibrant, salty approach to spirituality. It combines deep surrender with a gutsy, unflappable presence.

Mary was a New Yorker through and through, from her Brooklyn accent to her "in your face" kind of pizzazz. A divorced Catholic back in the era when such things were virtually unheard of, she supported her family through her job as an administrator in a psychiatric hospital, later offering her spare time as a literacy volunteer in the prisons. Through her work in therapy she was familiar with the "biofeedback" techniques then sprouting, and on her own she had already begun to develop a personal life practice combining these techniques with an underlying attitude of surrender that had been deeply imprinted on her through reading *Abandonment to Divine Providence*, a seventeenth-century spiritual classic by Pierre de Caussade. When she encountered Centering Prayer and Thomas Keating's evolving teachings on the false self system, the pieces began to come together for her in a single, integrated method.

The Welcoming Prayer was first taught at Chrysalis House, in Warwick, New York, Contemplative Outreach's first experiment in contemplative living, which she helped found. Several of the community members, particularly David Frenette and Cathy McCarthy, contributed to the fine-tuning. The practice proved so successful in bringing about real inner change that it was soon being offered far more widely throughout the network.

## How Does It Work?

As I mentioned earlier, the Welcoming Prayer works in active life with exactly the same place that Centering Prayer works in meditation: that slim window of opportunity before "thoughts" proceed to "passions."

Like most methods of inner awakening, it operates on the principle of making a separation between the "I" totally lost in its reactions, desires, and aversions and the deeper "I." But it does this in a very unique and interesting way. Rather than simply letting go of the thought, as is done in Centering Prayer itself and in many schools of inner work, it actually "rides" the gathering storm of emotional and physical energy that has already started to build by the time a person becomes conscious of frustration. Essentially it redirects the pathway of this energy through the body so that it is liberated from the false self system and recaptured as vital energy for inner transformation. It is a vibrant energetic practice, which is one of the main reasons its results are so dramatic and effective.

The ideal time to practice is as close to "ground zero" as possible—as soon as possible after you become aware of that initial sense of "frustration" arising (point **5A** on the diagram). This is not always feasible, of course. Sometimes, such as in the middle of that clash with your boss, you can't simply slip away to go do your Welcoming Prayer. There is nothing to do except to wave goodbye to yourself as you go over the waterfall, then pick up the pieces as soon afterward as you can. The practice does take some actual physical time to do, particularly in the beginning while you're still learning the moves. But with practice and dedication, you'll discover that the time required tends to diminish—and your conscious awareness increases—so the practice can be done almost simultaneously with the perceived upset itself.

Since it's easier to do so, I'll start by applying the process to afflictive emotions. Later we'll see how the same process can be applied to those "peacock feathers," as they were called in my own inner work group: the false positives achieved by *appeasement* of the false self programs. The practice is also highly effective in working with physical pain.

At any rate, whether positive or negative is the issue in question, the three-step process is as follows below:
1. Focus and Sink In
2. Welcome
3. Let Go

## Focus and Sink In

To focus on the upset means to feel it *as sensation in your body*. If it is a physical pain, like a toothache or backache, you become very present to it, putting your full attention inside it. Exactly the same is true for emotional upset. If you are angry, see if you can be present to how anger is manifesting in you. Is your jaw clenched? Is your stomach in knots? If fear is present, what is the *sensation* of fear? See if you can pay attention to what it feels like inside you. Is your breath short? Is there a sense of vertigo, or a stampede of "fight or flight" adrenaline?

Don't try to change anything. Just stay present.

Please keep in mind that focusing does *not* mean psychoanalyzing yourself, trying to discover why you feel the way you do, or justifying your feelings. When you are really upset, trying to psychoanalyze yourself is like pouring oil on fire anyway; it only tends to exacerbate the sensation. More significantly, from the perspective of inner work, self-analysis lands you right back in your egoic self, while staying with sensation will align you with your inner observer.

The importance of this step is really paramount; in fact, it holds the key to the entire practice. By becoming physically aware of this energy as sensation in your body, you have avoided one of the major potential pitfalls of working with the inner observer: dissociation.

Dissociation—or to situate it within its more general psychological category, *repression*—is one of the primary occupational hazards of people on a spiritual path. Perhaps because of the idealism inherent in the path itself, the tendency is strong in spiritual seekers to want to "make a religion of one's better moments," and if you have been brought up (as I was) in a household where the expression of anger was unacceptable, you may be able to whisk it into your unconscious so quickly you don't even register that you are angry! From the point of view of authentic spiritual transformation, repression is not only useless but counterproductive, for that unrecognized anger simply goes right back down into your body, where it becomes just so much more sludge in the pipes blocking the free flow of your being. Spiritual practice in which separation is too mental—i.e., in which the inner observer is used primarily to dissociate from the unpleasant feelings rather than to experience and integrate them—will require some difficult unlearning somewhere along the line before inner integration is finally achieved. By keeping a firm grounding in physical sensation, the Welcoming Prayer ensures that this mistake is not made.

## Welcome

Now comes the most inscrutable and counterintuitive instruction in the whole method. Sitting there, steeped in the whole roiling sensation of your upset, you begin to say, ever so gently, "Welcome, anger" (or whatever the emotion is), "Welcome anger." If it's physical pain, the same drill applies: "Welcome, pain, welcome . . ."[2]

How's that again? If this intrusive, upsetting emotion is what necessitated the practice in the first place, why are we welcoming it? Isn't the goal to get rid of it?

Actually, no. The goal is not to let it chase you out of presence.

Admittedly, this teaching is paradoxical. Common sense tells you that the unruly emotion is the problem and the solution is to eliminate it. But by welcoming it instead, you create an atmosphere of inner hospitality. By embracing the thing you once defended yourself against or ran from, you are actually disarming it, removing its power to hurt you or chase you back into your smaller self.

There is a wonderful fantasy novel by Ursula Le Guin called *A Wizard of Earthsea*, which is actually an extended meditation on exactly this point.[3] A young wizard named Ged is in training to become a sorcerer. One day, horsing around with his friends, he inadvertently conjures up a minor demon. The demon proceeds to haunt him throughout the book. As he grows in power and influence, it grows right along with him. Gradually it turns very dark and begins to stalk him; he flees in terror. He runs to a city by the sea, but it follows him there. He hires a boat and rows out into the sea, but it follows him there. Finally he jumps into the water, but the thing is still right on his back. Finally, with all escape routes blocked, he does the only thing left to him: He turns to the demon and embraces it. At which point it vanishes, integrated back inside him as the shadow he is finally willing to own.

Ged's experience of liberation is the practical wisdom behind this mysterious second step in the Welcoming process. *This* moment can always be endured, the well-known contemporary spiritual writer Gerald May reminds us,[4] and the act of welcoming anchors us firmly in the Now. In terms of inner observer practice as we described it in the last chapter, this is the moment of unconditional presence, the moment where those two great streams, awareness and surrender, converge. The small self is surrendered into the inner observer, which allows you to remain connected with magnetic center and hence rightly aligned to receive the divine assistance that is always flowing toward you. In this configuration, you are able to stay present in the Now *regardless of its physical or psychological content*. It is a secret the great saints and mystics have always known.

So have the small birds perched on an electric wire. No matter how high the voltage, the energy will do you no harm as long as you don't give it a pathway to the ground (which is what identification really is, seen from an energetic perspective).

A couple of important clarifications are in order. First of all, what you are welcoming is *the physical or psychological content of the moment only*, not a general blanket condoning of a situation. I am frequently asked by people with abuse histories, "But incest shouldn't be welcomed, should it?" This misses the point. What you are welcoming in this moment is not incest, but the *feelings* the experience triggers for you: the fear or rage or shame on your plate right now.

A friend of mine, well experienced in the practice, made this mistake; it is all too easy to do. A suspicious test caused her doctor to schedule her for a colonoscopy. "I tried to work with the Welcoming Prayer," she said, "but colon cancer is a hard thing to welcome."

Again, you can spot her error. What was on her plate in that moment was not cancer, but the *fear* of cancer. That was the situation she needed to be working with. It was not "Welcome, cancer," but "Welcome, fear."

This is a very important mistake to nip in the bud, because if uncorrected it can lead to the assumption that surrender means to roll over and play dead, or that the purpose of this practice is to teach you to passively acquiesce to situations that are in fact intolerable. This is not so at all. There is a crucial distinction between surrender as an inner attitude and as an outer practice, and we are concerned only with the former here. From the point of view of inner work, the situation is very straightforward: Anything done in a state of interior bracing will throw you immediately into your small self, with its familiar repertoire of defense mechanisms. Surrender understood as an interior act will place you in alignment with magnetic center, the seat of your inner observer, through which Divine Being can flow to you. Once you are in right alignment, you can *decide* what you are going to do in the outer world. Sometimes this is acquiescence, sometimes it is a spirited fight. But whichever way, you will be doing it from consciousness, not reactivity.

## Let Go

Don't get to this step too quickly. The real work in the Welcoming Prayer is actually accomplished in the first two steps. Stay with them—rather like kneading a charley horse in your leg—going back and forth between "focusing" and "welcoming" until the knot begins to dissolve of its own accord.

And yes, "letting go" is also just for now. This is not a final, forever renunciation of your anger or fear; it's simply a way of gently waving farewell as the emotion starts to recede. If you simply can't in good conscience move to this step, don't fake it; the bulk of the work has really been accomplished.

When you are ready to let go, there are two ways to go about it: a short way and a more complex litany. In the short way, you simply say something like "I let go of my anger," or, if you prefer, "I give my anger to God."

Mary Mrozowski, however, preferred a more complex and invariable litany. When it became time to proceed to the third step, she would use the following formula:

> I let go my desire for security and survival.
> I let go my desire for esteem and affection.
> I let go my desire for power and control.
> I let go my desire to change the situation.

This would be her inevitable litany, whether dealing with physical or emotional affliction. Those first three, of course, are the three false self programs, and in naming them thusly, Mary said, "I feel like I'm sending a strong message to the unconscious."

The last one, "I let go my desire to change the situation," is right between the eyeballs and a stroke of pure genius. In no uncertain terms, it removes this practice from the ballpark of "fix-it" ("I do my practice in order to correct an unpalatable situation") and back into unconditional presence. For Mary, this practice was all about correct inner alignment. Whether the pain went on forever was not the point; the point is that throughout this entire "forever," an awakened and surrendered consciousness can remain fully present to God—"for the duration."

## "Christ will storm the hell in you . . ."

Like most of these great practices on the spiritual path, the Welcoming Prayer is "simple but not easy." It can be a very wild ride, almost like a bucking bronco or a surfboard before a breaking wave. The surge of emotional energy can be strong as it courses through you. You are not trying to "back down" your emotions or talk yourself out of them, just to stay present to them from that deeper witnessing place.

What is most fascinating to me about this practice is how powerfully it frees up energy. We usually don't realize just how much of our vital life energy is bound up and unconsciously leached away in those "energy centers." One thing you may notice about that diagram is that the feedback loop is totally entropic; the energy generated in useless identified emotion simply gets reabsorbed into those unconscious false self programs. The energy of your being remains bound, at a frequency too slow and too self-preoccupied to sustain real inner awakening.

There's a classic saying in inner work: "As your Being increases, your receptivity to higher meaning increases. As your Being decreases, the old meanings return."[5]

A false self system is a system working at a low level of being, which is why it remains so mechanical and viciously self-reinforcing. With its vital energy largely locked up in its defenses and neurotic programming, there is little left over to reach escape velocity into real awakened consciousness, which both requires and produces a higher level of spiritual vibrancy than we are used to.

In the Welcoming Prayer the energy normally bound up in identification is suddenly vitally freed—sometimes so dramatically you can almost hear a "whoosh"—and the influx of this new energy is immediately experienced as a deepening and vitalization of your innermost being.

A friend of mine in Maine experienced this process very vividly. She had lost her husband a few months earlier to a painful and extremely fast-moving cancer. As she developed her strategy for managing her grief, she knew that early evening would be the hardest time of the day to get through, when she and her husband had been accustomed to sharing the events of the day with each other over a leisurely glass of wine. So she wisely scheduled a daily racket ball class for five p.m. to get her out of the house and physically active. It was a good idea. But late one February afternoon, a slashing ice storm came through, took out the power lines, and covered the roads with glare ice.

So there she was, alone in a dark house. But she was a staunch member of our spiritual journey group and decided that now would be as good a time as ever to work with the Welcoming Prayer. Sinking deeply into those places where the grief and pain lived within her, she slowly began saying, "Welcome, grief . . . welcome, grief . . . welcome, grief . . ."

"It was like day and night," she told me afterward. "One moment I couldn't stand it anymore; the next minute I could. If this grief were to go on forever, I knew that I could be with it the whole way. Whatever joined me in that moment is what it's really all about." Her open heart had catapulted her directly into the center of the Mystery of this prayer practice.

Nearly four centuries ago the German mystic Jacob Boehme described a practice very similar to the Welcoming Prayer in the following words:

> Here now, is the right place for you to wrestle before the divine face. If you remain firm, if you do not bend, you shall see and perceive great wonders. You will discover how Christ will storm the hell in you and will break your beasts. . . .[6]

It is interesting how for Boehme "remain firm and do not bend" is the exact equivalent of what I have been intending by the word *surrender*. It means to stand firm on both axes of your being (the horizontal and the vertical), without collapsing the tension and running back into that false self system feedback loop. He means "unconditional presence," which is what surrender really is, seen from the perspective of inner awakening. What then happens, according to him, is something truly wondrous: "You will discover how Christ will storm the hell in you and will break your beasts." In that wondrous moment, surrender and awareness come together in the explosion which is the Christ light going off in your own being. Sometimes it has such a force that you can actually feel it, as my friend did. But it is always there, this critical alchemy on the path of inner awakening that makes the Welcoming Prayer not simply about the healing of afflictive emotion, but a fundamental creation in you of something that was never there before. It is Christ illumining your darkness like the bush that burns but is not consumed, and in that moment you will begin to glimpse what true self is all about.

## Peacock Feathers

The obvious place to begin to work with this practice is in that area of the afflictive emotions. They're right in your face, and the pain they cause you is a strong motivator to do the practice. But if you want to use the practice for quantum inner awakening, give it a try as well on those so-called peacock feathers: those times when your ego is smugly glowing within its comfort zone, even if the satisfaction appears to you to be perfectly legitimate.

I remember vividly the first time it occurred to me to practice this way. I was coming home from a church meeting one night, in a happy afterglow because of a liturgical celebration that had gone particularly well. As I drove along, I found myself happily smelling all the little bouquets I'd collected: the liturgy itself, the smiling faces, the nice comments.

Suddenly, out of the deep, I heard an inner voice asking, "What do you *really* want in this moment? God or self-congratulation?" All of a sudden the atmosphere of my self began to feel uncomfortably close. Practicing as I'd learned to do, I focused in on where this feeling of self-satisfaction was living in my body, then began, "Welcome, pride, welcome pride . . ."

It was an interesting drill, to say the least. I noticed right away that somehow it is much harder to say "welcome, pride" than "welcome, loneliness" or "welcome, anger." But as I kept up the practice, I could feel the inner atmosphere shift, and the state of self-satisfaction giving way to a deeper equanimity.

And equanimity is the state we're aiming for, of course. As we've discussed earlier, the essential difference between psychological work and bona fide inner awakening is that the former tries to maximize gain on the pain/pleasure principle, whereas inner work tries to free you from that cycle altogether. You find your real comfort zone in a consciousness completely at home in itself and completely at home in God, regardless of the outside circumstances.

While the Welcoming Prayer was originally conceived more in the therapeutic mode, as a practical tool to extend the surrender of Centering Prayer into daily life by the "letting go" of afflictive emotions, it more than holds its own as a tool of inner awakening, and used with this deliberate intention, it can take you all the way there. It is the most potent practice I know to engage the attention of the heart and apply it to the total transformation of consciousness.

## Mary's Story

Mary Mrozowski herself traveled this path to the end; in fact, in some ways the last decade of her life was an increasingly go-for-broke experiment in just how far the Welcoming Prayer could take you.

On her long-awaited first trip to Italy, her expectations were suddenly turned completely upside down when a car hurtling out of control ran up on the sidewalk, slammed into her, and pinned her against a wall. In the midst of intense pain and a madhouse of confusion, she was able to keep saying, "Welcome, pain, welcome pain, welcome pain," and to recite unflappingly the litany, "I let go my desire to change the situation." Her calm was not only amazing but actually contagious; the crowd began to calm down. And while the story is probably apocryphal, one version has it that although she spoke little or no Italian, she was able to find the words to say, "Call for emergency help."

Watching her in those last years was like watching a home-grown saint emerging before one's very eyes, Brooklyn accent and all. She continued giving workshops on the Welcoming Prayer, which drew increasingly large crowds as word got out that Mary had definitely come of age as a spiritual teacher. Her insights and responses were delivered from that place of authentic authority that only emerges out of a lifetime of "walking the walk."

A huge crowd was gathered for the Contemplative Outreach conference in Denver in October 1993, and Mary's talk didn't disappoint. Sparkling and peppery as always, she had the audience on its feet! The enthusiastic crowd pressed in on her as she attempted to leave the speaker's podium, and she was knocked backward onto a lower platform, hitting her head. She insisted it was nothing, and rapidly picked herself up and continued the workshop. Then she headed home for dinner and an evening with her host, Sister Bernadette Teasdale, before delivering her final talk the next day.

That next morning, as she was sitting in an armchair giving spiritual direction to Sister Bernadette, suddenly a jolt swept through her body and she lost consciousness and slid to the floor. Recovering briefly, she opened her eyes and asked, "What happened?" Then she passed out again. Those were her final words.

"Welcome death . . . welcome death . . . welcome death . . ." Not in spoken words but in the gentleness of her acceptance the meaning was eloquently clear. "For I am convinced that neither death nor life, neither angels nor demons . . . nor anything else in all creation will be able to separate me from the love of God that is in Christ Jesus our Lord." That gesture of surrender, patterned into every fiber of her being, became the bridge on which she crossed.

# 14 ⑥ Centering Prayer and Christian Life

I have spoken so far of Centering Prayer as being rooted and grounded in *kenosis*, the self-emptying love of Christ understood as the core gesture of his life and the source of his sacramental power. But in Christian mystical theology, the word *kenosis* is used in another context as well: to describe the internal life of the Trinity. It speaks of the self-emptying love with which the Father spills into (or gives himself fully into) the Son, the Son into the Spirit, the Spirit into the Father. This complete intercirculation in love is called *perichoresis*. It's sort of like the buckets on a watermill; as they empty one into the other, the mill turns and the energy of love becomes manifest and accessible.

The same analogy I believe holds true for our life in God. What we experience in Centering Prayer as kenosis, or personal self-emptying, is always part and parcel of a greater perichoresis, one self-emptying spilling into another in the great watermill of love, through which God shows us his innermost nature and bestows this vital energy upon the world in a cascade of divine creativity.

"I am the vine; you are the branches; abide in me as I in you"

(John 15: 3–4). The most profoundly beautiful imagery in the New Testament is communal; it speaks of this great intercirculation of love. So often we think of Centering Prayer—or any form of meditation—as alone, withdrawn, or focused on one's own personal development or special relationship with God, not shared with others (because we're under the impression that the only way to share with others is to talk). But in point of fact, whenever we participate in that act of kenosis, it is always as part and parcel of perichoresis. That is the essential Mystery, the beauty that Jesus lived and died and through which he rose again. There is no gesture more ultimately communal than  kenosis, for it is the ultimate act of self-transcendence. As we participate in this gesture, no matter how isolated it first may feel, how divided and cut off from others, the deep truth we will eventually come to know is that any act of kenosis reconnects us, inevitably and instantly, to that great vine of love.

Thomas Merton learned this lesson through a long and difficult journey, perhaps the only way that this lesson is ever fully learned. When he entered the Abbey of Our Lady of Gethsemane in December 1941, the one thing he knew for certain was that he wanted out of "the world" and straight into God. As he took one last backward look before the monastery gate clanked shut behind him (he hoped forever), all he could see was a hopeless wasteland of sin, hypocrisy, noise, and illusion. Ahead lay a vast Himalayan silence and holiness. Or so he thought.[1]

But the contemplative life is full of its own surprising plot twists. Once you give yourself fully to it, once you sign on the dotted line of kenosis, perichoresis is what you'll eventually get. Seventeen years later, that inexorable inner blueprint bore fruit in him in a completely unexpected way, when, on a routine shopping trip into town he was suddenly engulfed in a blinding epiphany of love. He describes the experience in an essay movingly titled "A Member of the Human Race":

> In Louisville, at the Corner of Fourth and Walnut, in the center of the shopping district, I was suddenly over-

whelmed with the realization that I loved all those people, that they were mine and that I theirs, that we could not be alien to one another even though we were total strangers. It was like waking from a dream of separateness, of a pure self-isolation in a special world, the world of renunciation and supposed holiness.[2]

Nor was this a fluke "mystical experience." What Merton saw in that moment stayed with him till the end of his life; it was a permanent transformation of his consciousness. This is the unitive seeing we are all called to: the secret of Jesus' great commandment to "love your neighbor as yourself." Not *as much as* yourself, as egoic consciousness always interprets, but *as yourself*: interchangeably One in that great vine of love which is the mystical body of Christ.

If you embrace a path that begins in kenosis, you will wind up in perichoresis; that's the wager. That's also the Church—its vision and its path in a nutshell.

In October 2003 Thomas Keating convened a council of contemplative "elders" at St. Benedict's Monastery in Snowmass. The purpose of the meeting was to ponder ways to encourage a more thorough contemplative formation within the curriculum of seminaries, or in other words, in the training of future church leaders. Those invited to the meeting represented the three major "schools" of Christian meditation practice (Centering Prayer, Christian Zen, Christian Meditation) and virtually the entire spectrum of Christian denominational affiliations, from Roman Catholic to Baptist. What this diverse group of meditators had in common was years and years of experience in their respective practices.

As they sat down to the task, the group decided that it needed to begin by putting together a working definition of contemplative prayer and practice. By a process of group sharing and consensus, the twelve participants pooled their collective experience and came up with the following statement:

The Gospel is the core of Christian living. It has within it a contemplative dimension. This dimension is God's invitation to every human being, through Jesus Christ, to share God's very nature. It begins as a way of listening with ears, eyes, and heart. It grows as a desire to know God and to enter into God's love. This is made possible by a dying to self or emptying to self that becomes a radical emptying to God and experience of God's love. Through a pattern of abiding in God that we call contemplative prayer, a change of consciousness takes place. This dynamic sharing of God's nature forms each person and opens them to the mind and very life of Christ, challenging them to be instruments of God's love and energy in the world. This contemplative consciousness bonds each person in a union with God and with all other persons. It enables them to find God present in all things.[3]

What's striking about this statement is that the word "silence" isn't mentioned even once. Instead, what these mature contemplatives set their sights on is the radical transformation of the person! Contemplative practice for them is fundamentally about a change in consciousness that enables the practitioner to see and participate in the very nature of Christ. It is a bold way of saying "yes" to the profound invitation of Ephesians 3:18–19: ". . . that rooted and grounded in love [you] may come to grasp how wide and long and high and deep is the love of Christ—that you may be filled with the very nature of God."

You would think, being contemplative masters, that these group members would specify how much and what kind of silence constitutes a minimum prerequisite for transformation. But they don't. Contemplative prayer itself is merely loosely defined as "a pattern of abiding in God." The thing that actually does the trick is "the dying to self or emptying to self that is a radical opening to God."

Nor does contemplation have anything to do with "a life apart" or even, as in that celebrated motto of the hermit path, "separated from all, but united to all." Here it is simply "united to all." Whether that unity is lived out in physical reclusion or in the trenches doesn't really matter; it's the union that counts.

What makes this statement so interesting is that it displaces just about every available sacred cow that would allow us to think of contemplative prayer as some sort of "life apart," at the opposite extreme from a life of action or Christian engagement. If anything it's just the opposite. Contemplative prayer, when it becomes full and mature, doesn't widen the gap between prayer and life; it narrows it. Both prayer and life flow out of and give authentic expression to that same "dying to self or emptying to self that is a radical opening to God."

Along the learning curve silence is useful, or course, but not for the reason that most of us might think. It's not that silence is in itself pious, holy, or closer to God. We tend to picture God as a wild, wary thing, at home only in the ineffable; if we're extremely silent, he may cautiously approach. But it's not like this at all. The reality is that God is always present, and we're the ones who are absent! We hide in the cataphatic: in our noise, our stories, our self-talking, our busyness. Silence is useful in that it takes away the evasions; it forces us to befriend our own consciousness and stop running from our own shadows. Once that willingness has been found—the willingness simply to endure ourselves in the present moment—then the external conditions of silence become much less important. I've seen Thomas Keating do his Centering Prayer in the middle of an airline terminal! On the other hand, without that consent to fully inhabit ourselves, even silence itself will soon get piled high with rules, self-definitions, rigidity, and piety; it becomes itself a form of evasion.

What in most people begins as an "attraction to silence" is really, at root, a desire to end the evasion. Like the character Ged in the novel *A Wizard of Earthsea*, silence heralds the dawning inner recognition that the thing you've been running from all your life is really *you*; you have to turn and embrace it. That fundamental turn is what contemplative life is built on and what silence celebrates and honors: the realization that who and what you are can neither be exhausted nor fulfilled in that endless cycle of doing, running, desiring, and demanding. As Jesus so long ago taught, "The Kingdom of Heaven is within you."

Of course, when you're first trying to establish a meditation practice (and for a long while afterward), it looks like a huge arm-wrestle with time: trying to find a way to shoehorn those one or two periods of Centering Prayer into a day already overscheduled and overcommitted. I remember an introductory workshop I once taught where one of the participants was a young mother of three preschoolers. When I went through the talk on how Centering Prayer is about letting go of all thoughts, she remarked, "I'm going to be a natural at this! I haven't had a thought in years!" But the promise contemplative prayer makes is that if you show up, things will start to change. Not in the way you expect, of course, but change they will. That "thing" you embraced when you stopped fleeing will begin to quicken within you. And while everybody's journey is different, the general direction—as those contemplative elders made clear—is that rather than pulling you out of life, it will deposit you back in the midst of it, with a soft and warm heart and a deepening sense of wonder.

The goal of contemplative life is unitive seeing: not so much "union with God" understood as wanting God to the exclusion of all else, but rather, gradually coming to realize that really, there is nothing that is *not* God. God is the higher and the lower, the dots and the spaces between the dots; nothing can fall out of God, and all is tenderly and joyously held. To see this is to behold the Kingdom here and now and to be in constantly renewed immediacy with the source of your own true abundance. The goal of the contemplative life, then, is to make "beautiful Christians": those with the insight and the inner flexibility to flow into life in any and all circumstances knowing that the fountainhead is love.

For me this has everything to do with the Church.

What I am suggesting here (and of course, what those contemplative elders were driving at, too) is that the contemplative dimension, thus repositioned away from the traditional stereotypes of cloistered monasteries, gobs of silence, and otherworldliness, is really Christianity's missing "path": its way of getting from here to there. Contemplative prayer reflects a long and noble lineage of Christians who have attempted to "put on the mind of Christ"—not just through outer works or even "faith alone," but through a radical transformation of consciousness that produces the Kingdom as its fruit. Applying Jesus' teaching that "a house divided against itself cannot stand," they have striven to heal their own divided and warring consciousnesses and bring their lives into an inner alignment through which it becomes possible to actually *follow* the teachings of Christ (which are in fact pitched to a level of consciousness higher than the egoic) and to live them into reality with integrity and grace. Ever since that first great contemplative "experiment" in the deserts of Egypt and Syria, the goal has been radical transformation of the human person in service of the Kingdom. It doesn't require an "introverted temperament"— only honesty, commitment, and a good sense of humor. From these three raw ingredients, great saints can be fashioned.

The contemporary theologian Marcus Borg has made a fascinating suggestion: that the word *metanoia*, commonly translated as "repent," actually means to "go beyond the mind," or "go into the larger mind."[4] In a nutshell this is what the contemplative journey is all about. The wager is that when we actually enter that larger mind, our "apophatic," or spiritual, mind, we discover that it is neither empty nor a void; it dances with the living water of love, tumbling as it has from time out of time, in that great perichoresis of Father—Son—Holy Spirit through which the "love that moves the stars and the sun" is generated and sustained. At the center of our own being is Being itself, and in this we are ultimately sustained and come to know ourselves as we truly are.

I end this book where I began it: nearly half a century ago, as a young child sitting in Quaker meeting. In the profundity yet utter simplicity of that silent worship, my Christian life began. Somehow, with an eloquence I have never forgotten, I met and came to know in that silence the vine that all the branches went down into. Perhaps because of that early imprinting, I have always thought

159

of contemplative prayer first and foremost as *worship in community*. While it is often, perhaps even typically, practiced alone or in small home gatherings, I believe that its true home is the Church, the steward in this world of the intertwining Mysteries of kenosis and perichoresis. If I have spent so much time in this book trying to allay the fears and hesitation of Christians who might regard this prayer as in any way alien, it is because I have seen with my own eyes the beauty and power of the Christianity that emerges when the two streams are reunited and lived together as a single whole. Silence and the Word: healing, transforming, creating in the full vibrancy of love.

# Epilogue  The Way of the Heart

According to an old preaching class joke, the standard recipe for constructing a sermon goes something like this: "First tell them what you're about to tell them, then tell them it, then tell them you've told them." At the risk of that same sort of redundancy, I thought it might be useful to summarize some of the most important points I've made about Centering Prayer over the course of this book. Condensed into a kind of "top ten" list, they serve as a quick overview of Centering Prayer from the angle that I've been approaching it: as a comprehensive method for inner awakening.

While most of what I'll share here is review, you'll find a few new ideas here as well, which I hope you'll find intriguing. At any rate, here are my "top ten" (twelve, actually). Ponder them at your leisure.

As a method of meditation, Centering Prayer is founded upon the gesture of surrender, or letting go. The theological basis for this prayer lies in the principle of *kenosis* (Philippians 2:6), Jesus' self-

161

emptying love that forms the core of his own self-understanding and life practice. During the prayer time itself, surrender is practiced through the letting go of thoughts as they arise. Unlike other forms of meditation, neither focused awareness nor a steady witnessing presence is required. There is no need to "follow" the thoughts as they arise; merely to let them go promptly as soon as you realize you're engaged in thinking (a "Sacred Word" is typically used to facilitate this prompt release).

This gesture of prompt release is *physically embodied*. It is not just an attitude; something actually "drops and releases" in the solar plexus region of your body, a subtle but distinct form of inner breathing. Thus, prayer periods in which your inner atmosphere is not particularly quiet (where there are a lot of thoughts and a lot of letting go) are not "bad" meditations, although that may be your subjective experience of them if you have the preconception that a "good" meditation is one where there's lots of stillness. Those more athletic sits are a good "aerobic workout" for that "muscle" of surrender.

With committed practice, this well-patterned gesture of release begins to coalesce as a distinct "magnetic center" within you. In and of its own accord, it begins to hold you at that place of deeper spiritual attentiveness during prayer time. Thoughts still come and go, but you have little attraction to grab onto them. Magnetic center keeps you firmly connected to your depths—in fact, sometimes it's flatly impossible to move out of its gravitational pull. Later, you will begin to feel its tug even when you are not in Centering Prayer, reminding you of that deepening life of prayer that's beginning to flow within you even as you move about the business of your daily life.

This "magnetic center" may feel like a homing beacon or a point of inner alignment, and in fact that's true. Today's sailors and navigators rely on a Global Positioning System (GPS) to keep them on course. You might think of magnetic center as another sort of GPS—a "God positioning system." It keeps the outer part of you aligned with that deeper center: your yearning for God and God's for you. Gradually you learn how to use it to thread your way among the competing claims and clamors of the outside world and the continuous undertow of the false self system. When the signal grows dim, or you forget to listen, it's a fairly safe bet that you've wandered off course.

"Magnetic center" is one way to describe this growing seat of internal alignment. But there is another way to describe it as well, which may at first surprise you. It is your *heart*.

In the modern West we are accustomed to thinking of the heart as the center of our personal emotional life and affectivity, but in the classic traditions of inner awakening, this is not so. The heart is first and foremost an organ of spiritual perception.

The modern Sufi master Kabir Helminski gives a succinct description of the heart as it has been classically understood in the Western inner spiritual tradition:

> We have subtle subconscious faculties we are not using. Beyond the limited analytic intellect is a vast realm of mind that includes psychic and extrasensory abilities; intuition; wisdom; a sense of unity; aesthetic, qualitative and creative faculties; and image-forming and symbolic capacities. Though these faculties are many, we give them a single name with some justification because they are operating best when they are in concert. They comprise a mind, moreover, in spontaneous connection with the cosmic mind. This total mind we call "heart."[1]

In this beautiful definition, emphasis is placed on the heart's capacity to create a spontaneous inner alignment between the human individual and the "cosmic mind," or God. Its job is to look deeper than the surface of things, deeper than that jumbled, reactive landscape of ordinary awareness, and to beam in on that deeper, ensheltering spiritual world in which our being is rooted. As the heart becomes strong and clear and you are able to follow its promptings reliably, you come into alignment with divine Being and are able to live authentically out of your true self.

This is why, across the board in the three Abrahamic traditions (Judaism, Christianity, and Islam), the heart is seen as the core of the human person, the uniquely precious expression of his or her essence. That is true. But it is not because the heart, per se, is the authentic human being, but because in its role as the aligning agent, it allows that authentic being to manifest.

Centering prayer, then, can be looked on as a methodology par excellence for nurturing the heart. This is the ballpark in which it works and against which its effectiveness must be measured. Most traditional methods of meditation aim for clarity of mind. Centering prayer aims for purity (or in other words, "singleness") of heart.

The term *putting the mind in the heart* comes specifically from Eastern Orthodox spirituality, but the concept is foundational to both Eastern and Western spiritual theologies (which share a common root in the spirituality of the Desert). By whatever name, it represents one of the grand goals of the Christian mystical path. Traditionally, this is accomplished by a "concentration of affectivity"—or in other words, by fanning the flames of the heart's native capacity for empathy, then concentrating this aroused emotion on the love of God. Centering Prayer follows a different tack. Building on an insight first articulated by Simeon the New Theologian (949–1022), it suggests that "putting the mind in the heart" can be accomplished just as effectively through kenosis, or the simple release of whatever you are clinging to. Thus, Centering Prayer represents an alternative way of "getting from here to there." Putting the mind in the heart is accomplished not from "top down" but from "bottom up," through releasing the passions and relaxing the will. The approach is untraditional but completely orthodox.

One of the most important side effects of following this "bottom up" route is that it produces changes not only in the conscious realm but in the unconscious as well. Thomas Keating's most original contribution to contemporary spiritual psychology lies in the realization that the profound receptivity in the method of Centering Prayer relaxes the repressive tendencies of the ego and encourages a release of the pain, neurotic defenses, and "emotional wounds" of a lifetime carried in the unconscious. Rather than seeing meditation as a tool for developing concentration, relaxing stress, or accessing higher states of consciousness, he sees it primarily as a catalyst for "the purification of the unconscious." It is important for practitioners of Centering Prayer to keep in mind that it is not only a devotional method but a psychological one as well and will produce effects in this realm.

This purification is itself prayer, Keating emphasizes: not a preparation for relationship with God, but the relationship itself. He calls this relationship "the divine therapy," recognizing that the "transference" (i.e., a deepening trust and sense of safety) experienced during prayer encourages this psychological healing to happen, and that as healing occurs, a person's relationship to God grows and deepens as well. This "apophatic psychotherapy" does not necessarily replace the need for traditional psychotherapy, but it reinforces it through a deepening spiritual dimension. The fruits of this journey are seen not only in profound healing at the psychological level, but in the gradual emergence of "the contemplative gifts of the spirit," whose earmarks are compassion, humility, and a growing equanimity.

In and of itself, a life of continuous and deepening surrender brings about a profound transformation in the psyche: a deepening and gentling of the human being. But the transformation is vastly accelerated when Centering Prayer is combined with a practice of "inner observation," or "witnessing presence," as is taught in traditional schools of inner awakening (and in most forms of meditation). Once the process is under way, it becomes clear that Centering Prayer provides an even more solid foundation for this work than traditional forms of inner observer practice (which can become too mental) because in Centering Prayer the witnessing presence, or "inner observer," is easily and naturally carried in magnetic center.

The Welcoming Prayer practice, Centering Prayer's most powerful tool for carrying prayer into daily life, is even more effective as an awareness practice (not just a surrender practice) and when used in this way results in quantum growth toward "unitive" consciousness.

Traditional spiritual practice tends to envision dismantling the ego (or "false self system," in Thomas Keating's rendition) as a necessary prerequisite in the evolution toward unitive consciousness; "true self" is what emerges after the egoic system has been dismantled. But if you trust the process of Centering Prayer, you'll begin to see that it's not really necessary or even helpful to put your focus on dismantling the false self. Instead, your emphasis need only be on *nurturing the heart* through the threefold practices of (1) surrender during the prayer time, (2) surrender/awareness carried into daily life through work with the Welcoming Prayer, and (3) regular participation in some form of Christian liturgical community, which will keep you grounded in the Mystical Body of Christ and feed you with the direct soul food of the Eucharist and sacred scripture.

As you nurture the heart, your ego will begin to relativize of its own accord. It can then do its real job as a useful instrument of manifestation—in the same way a violin lets you manifest the music. But you have come to know that you are not your violin.

# Notes

### Chapter 1: Contemplative Prayer and Centering Prayer

1. John of the Cross wrote, "The Father spoke one word from all eternity and he spoke it in silence, and it is in silence that we hear it." Commenting on this passage, Thomas Keating observes: "This suggests that silence is God's first language and that all other languages are poor translations." Thomas Keating, *Intimacy with God* (New York: Crossroad, 1994), p. 55.

### Chapter 2: Deeper Silence, Deeper Self

1. See ahead, Chapter 6.
2. Matthew Fox, ed., *Breakthrough: Meister Eckhart's Creation Spirituality in New Translation* (New York: Image Books, 1980), p. 126.
3. Thomas Merton, *A Merton Reader*, ed. Thomas P. McDonnell (New York: Image Books, 1989), p. 347.

### Chapter 3: The Method of Centering Prayer

1. It is probably not by coincidence that the same deep "ah" of the "Om" sound —widely regarded in the East as the primordial vibration of creation—continues to resonate through Christian prayer words such as *alleluia, amen, Abba,* and *Maranatha.*
2. Ira Progoff, ed., *The Cloud of Unknowing* (New York: Delta Books, 1957), p. 76. It should be noted that in Centering Prayer terminology the word *thought* is used in a very broad way to cover any sense perception at all. It includes not only mental activity, but also bodily sensations, feeling, reflections, memories, images, and spiritual experiences. See ahead, Chapter 4.

### Chapter 4: Handling Thoughts during Prayer Time

1. I first encountered this wonderful image from Rumi in a song cycle called *Rumi: Songs of Divine Love,* composed by Ray Vincent Adams, which had its world première in Aspen, Colorado, on February 14, 2001. The short poems comprising the libretto were mostly taken from *The Essential Rumi,* translated by Coleman Barks (HarperSanFrancisco, 1995), though I have been as yet unable to locate this verse within that particular collection.
2. Fr. Tom Francis, "Centering Prayer," pamphlet prepared for retreatants at the Monastery of the Holy Spirit, Conyers, Georgia. Shared with me through personal correspondence in January 2003.

### Chapter 5: Spiritual Non-Possessiveness

1. The temptations in the wilderness are described in parallel versions in Matthew 4 and Luke 4. For an insightful commentary by a contemporary spiritual master, see *The New Man* by Maurice Nicoll (New York: Penguin Books, 1976), pp. 19–31. The confrontation at Jesus' arrest is in Matthew 26:52. When one of Jesus' companions attempts to defend him, he commands, "Put your sword back in its place. Do you think I

cannot call on my Father, and he will at once put at my disposal more than twelve legions of angels? But how then would Scripture be fulfilled that says it must happen in this way?"

2. Sogyal Rinpoche, *The Tibetan Book of Living and Dying* (San Francisco: HarperSanFrancisco, 1992).

3. Evelyn Underhill, *Mysticism* (New York: Dutton, 1961), p. 247.

4. Rabindranath Tagore, *Collected Poems and Plays* (Towbridge, U.K.: Macmillan, 1973), p. 188.

5. The teaching is developed most extensively in the Sufi tradition, where these subtle centers of perception are known as the *lataif*. For a good general introduction, see A.H. Almaas, *Spacecruiser Inquiry* (Boston: Shambhala, 2002), pp. 253–57; or Kabir Helminski, *The Knowing Heart* (Boston: Shambhala, 1999), pp. 80–82. Please note that these are not the same as the chakras, which are energy centers; the *lataif* work with qualities of consciousness more subtle than physical energy. Some authors refer to this more subtle level as "psychic force": the realm of qualities such as attention, love, and will.

6. The first quotation is from Thomas Merton, *Contemplation in a World of Action* (New York: Image Books, 1967), p. 299. The second is taken from an unpublished manuscript shared with me by the monks of St. Benedict's Monastery in Snowmass, Colorado. Much of this essay was later published in a series called "The Contemplative Experience," which ran in several successive issues of *The Cistercian Review* during 1983.

## Chapter 6: Centering Prayer and Christian Tradition

1. TM is the acronym for Transcendental Meditation, one of the most popular of these Eastern hybrids that was brought to North America in the early 1960s by Maharishi Mahesh Yogi.

2. To this triumvirate of Benedictines should appropriately be added a fourth: Fr. Bede Griffiths, whose search for the contemplative dimension, which he called "the other half of my soul," led him to India, where he founded Shantivanam Ashram, a place of deep and nurturing communion between Western and Eastern paths to the center. While less well known in North America than Merton, Keating, and Main, his contribution is no less important, and the significance of his pioneering work is steadily gaining recognition.

3. *The Cloud of Unknowing: Introductory Translation and Commentary by Ira Progoff* (New York: Delta Books, 1957), p. 76. While the most popular edition of *The Cloud* is by William Johnston (New York: Doubleday, 1973), Progoff's translation is in my opinion considerably more accurate and helpful because of his acute psychological understanding of the "Work" (the term used by the author of *The Cloud*) of inner awakening. Progoff developed the proprioceptive method of journaling widely in use in contemporary spiritual direction and therapeutic practice.

4. Contemplative Outreach can be contacted at P.O. Box 737—10 Park Place, Suite 2B, Butler, NJ 07405; telephone 973-838-3384; email office@coutreach.org; website: www.contemplativeoutreach.org.

5. In fact, the word *obedience* in its authentic etymological sense means exactly this. It comes from the Latin *ob-audire*, which means "to listen

deeply, or from the depths."

6. Recovery of the Syriac traditions has been one of the most important scholarly accomplishments of our times, creating a very different picture of both the theology and spiritual practices of early Christianity from what we are accustomed to in the Christian West. For a good starting point, see Sebastian Brock, ed., *The Syriac Fathers on Prayer and the Spiritual Life*, (Kalamazoo, MI: Cistercian Press, 1987).

   On prayer in secret, consider the following text, an eleventh-century record of practices stemming from a group of ninth- and tenth-century Sufi mystics. The passage is taken from Sara Sviri, *The Taste of Hidden Things* (Inverness, CA: The Golden Sufi Center, 1997), p. 134:

   "One of their principles maintains four levels of the remembrance of God—the *dhikr* (remembrance) of the tongue, the *dhikr* of the heart, the *dhikr* of the 'secret' *(sirr)*, and the *dhikr* of the spirit *(ruh)* . . . Each of these levels has a blemish. The blemish of the *dhikr* of the spirit is that it is perceived by the secret. The blemish of the *dhikr* of the heart is that the lower self might take notice and admire it, or that it might gain by it the reward of attaining a spiritual rank."

   I will return to this passage in Chapter 11, for it contains a key insight into an aspect of Centering Prayer that has troubled some teachers accustomed to more traditionally Eastern meditation methods: its willingness to let go of a clear "I am" presence, a watching consciousness that remains present to itself beneath the passing psychological phenomena.

7. What about the Lord's Prayer, then, which follows immediately afterward in Matthew's gospel? I join with those who believe that the Lord's Prayer is to be taken not simply (or even primarily) as a spoken prayer, but as a *method* of prayer: a set of underlying attitudes toward God, neighbor, and life that are to be practiced in every moment of life. The method of Centering Prayer certainly corresponds to and develops proficiency in sustaining this attitude. See ahead, to Chapter 8.

8. Benedicta Ward, ed., *The Desert Christian: The Sayings of the Desert Fathers* (New York: Macmillan, 1975), pp. 1–2.

9. In the Rule of St. Benedict, for example, we find the following instruction about monastic psalmody: "For monks who in a week's time say less than the full psalter betray extreme indolence and lack of devotion in their service. We read, after all, that our holy Fathers, energetic as they were, did all this in a single day." RSB, Chapter 18; quoted from *The Rule of St. Benedict* (Collegeville, MN: Liturgical Press, 1980), p. 215.

10. Ward, *The Desert Christian*, p. 64.

11. *Ibid.*, p. 131.

12. *John Cassian, Conferences*, trans. Colm Luibheid (Mahwah, NJ: Paulist Press [in The Classics of Western Christianity series], 1985), p. 133.

13. *Ibid.*, emphasis added.

14. This is the vivid metaphor used by Abba Joseph to suggest the ultimate goal of the path of spiritual awakening: "If you wish, you shall become all flame." *The Desert Christian*, p. 103.

15. I will have more to say about this deepening process and the enkindling of the visionary imagination in the following chapter.

## Chapter 7: The Loss and Recovery of the Christian Contemplative Tradition

1. I first heard it directly mentioned in an address given by Fr. Basil Pennington, one of the original founders of the method of Centering Prayer, to the Contemplative Outreach National Coordinators Conference in Chicago, July 2001.

2. There was also a Guigo I, who taught these same four elements of "spiritual exercise," but in the reverse order. For an excellent commentary, see Simon Tugwell, *Ways of Imperfection* (Springfield, IL: Templegate, 1985), pp. 93ff.

3. See in particular, "Three Methods of Attention and Prayer" in E. Kadloubovsky and G.E.H. Palmer, translators, *Writings from the Philokalia on Prayer of the Heart*, (London and Boston: Faber and Faber, 1951, 1992), pp. 158–59.

4. The former schema is preferred by Thomas Keating and most of the Trappist lineage; the latter follows more authoritatively from Henri de Lubac's magisterial work on Christian liturgy, *Medieval Exegesis* (Grand Rapids, MI: Eerdmans, 1998), and is vigorously espoused by the contemporary Camaldolese Benedictine monk and teacher Fr. Bruno Barnhart. In fact, the order and even the number of these "senses of scripture" varied considerably throughout the Patristic and Medieval periods.

5. For a more detailed exploration of this subject, see my *A Wisdom Way of Knowing* (San Francisco: Jossey-Bass, 2003).

6. For an insightful study of this conundrum, see James Arraj, *From St. John of the Cross to Us* (Chiloquin, OR: Inner Growth Books, 1999). Arraj describes his study as "The story of a 400-year-long misunderstanding and what it means to the future of Christian mysticism."

7. As Simon Tugwell comments (*Ways of Imperfection*, p. 96): "This does not mean that contemplation can be produced to order; in Guigo's view it depends on God's good pleasure, it is a 'grace' which God gives as and when he likes. It is, more strictly, only a 'quasi-effect of prayer', but it is not likely to be given to anyone who has not passed through the first three stages. God may occasionally 'take the bull by the horns' and as it were force some people to desire him even though they do not want to, by giving himself to them without waiting to be asked. But this is not normal and we should not presume on its happening; if we aspire to contemplation, we should 'do what belongs to us, namely to read and meditate on the law of God, and pray to him that he will help our weakness.'"

8. Essentially, mystical experience tends to be ecstatic, presuming a high degree of absorption in God and a transcendence (or loss) of the personal sense of "I am here" presence. Unitive seeing tends to be *enstatic*; the individual remains lucid, fully present, and capable of interacting in the physical realm.

9. Arraj, *From St. John of the Cross to Us*, pp. 222–23.

10. Barbara Brown Taylor, *The Luminous Web: Essays on Science and Religion* (Cambridge, MA: Cowley Publications, 2000), p. 74.

## Chapter 8: The Theology of Centering Prayer

1. The qualifier "for me" ("whoever loses his life for me will save it") is regarded by most Biblical scholars as a later interpolation.

2. I add this cautionary note because of a lingering impression in certain quarters of the Centering Prayer movement that this prayer, in and of itself, will melt the false self and deliver one into transforming union. This misapprehension, which has the effect of relegating Centering Prayer to simply a new form of Quietism, is vigorously refuted by Thomas Keating himself.

3. See in particular Jim Marion's fascinating *Putting on the Mind of Christ: The Inner Work of Christian Spirituality* (Charlottesville, VA: Hampton Roads, 2000), an ambitious and largely successful attempt to correlate the classic paradigm of the Christian spiritual journey ("purgative/illuminative/unitive") with the more recent roadmaps of conscious evolution pioneered by the brilliant contemporary metaphysician Ken Wilber.

4. The version of this text I am citing here is a translation by the monks of New Camaldoli Hermitage, Big Sur, California, in active use in their liturgical and devotional life. It was through many years of singing this hymn with the monks during Saturday night vespers that its deeper significance began to open to me. The introductory exhortation ("Let what was seen in Jesus also be seen in you") has been translated in a variety of ways, from the traditional "Let there be in you the same mind that was in Christ" to the accurate but much blander rendition of the New International Version: "Your attitude should be the same as Christ Jesus." The version I cite in the text comes from *The Christian Community Bible* (Ligouri, MO: Ligouri Publications, 1995), a recent and singularly beautiful translation from the Philippines.

5. Anders Nygren, *Agape and Eros*, trans. Philip S. Watson (London: SPCK, 1953).

6. On the classic monastic path of both the East and the West, this aim also specifically entails the practice of celibacy, i.e., the refraining from genital sexual expression and the redirection of the sexual energy toward the upward journey.

7. Karl Rahner, "Thoughts on the Theology of Christmas," *Theological Investigations* Volume III (New York: Herder and Herder), p. 32.

8. Rumi, *Mathnawi*, VI, 1967–70. Quoted from Kabir Helminski, *Living Presence* (New York: Putnam/Jeremy Tarcher, 1992), p. 142.

9. The sonnet alluded to is Number 73. While many Western Christians may be uncomfortable with the word *tantra*, having heard it only in the context of sexual eroticism, the actual meaning of both the word itself and the spiritual methodology it describes is far more profound, and far closer to the pulse of Christianity's real heartbeat than most of us would dare to realize. The key, I believe, to really understanding the nature of the path on which Jesus leads us lies in reclaiming an image of him as a master of tantra, perhaps the greatest master of all times.

   In the narrowest sense, of course, tantra is about physical orgasm. But orgasm itself, spiritually understood, is an expression of something far greater: of love that reaches oneness through complete vulnerability and self-expenditure on behalf of another. The modern Roman Catholic theologian Ladislaus Boros brilliantly captures this deeper meaning (and hence, the relationship between human and divine love) in a few deft sentences in his book *God Is with Us* (London: Burns and Oates, 1967): "The gift that is given in love is ultimately always the giver himself. . . . When two people say 'we' because love has made them one in reality, a new sphere of existence is created. . . . This new sphere of existence is not simply 'already there'; it comes into existence as the function of the free self-giving of one person to the other" (6–7). These comments seem to suggest profound links between tantra, kenosis, and *perichoresis*, the theological term used to describe the "self-emptying" of one divine Person into another in the Trinity, and hence the creative principle itself, and the wellspring of "heaven and earth and everything visible and invisible." See above in the text.

## Chapter 9: The Divine Therapy

1. The first three of these works have now been collected in a single volume called *Foundations for Centering Prayer and the Christian Contemplative Life* (New York: Continuum, 2002). For a full bibliography of Fr. Keating's works, see the bibliography at the end of this book.
2. Thomas Keating, in a personal interview in October 1994. Essentially the same comment appears in his book *Invitation to Love* (Rockport, MA: Element, 1992), p. 3.
3. *Ibid.*
4. Thomas Keating, *Intimacy with God* (New York: Crossroad, 1994), p. 98.

## Chapter 10: From Healing to Holiness

1. For an insider's look at this remarkable ministry, see Jens Soering, *The Way of the Prisoner* (New York: Lantern Books, 2003).
2. This confusion is accentuated by what seems to me to be a curious weakness in Keating's presentation to date. While he very helpfully teaches a practice for allowing the "afflictive emotions" to help uncover frustrated programs still strongly in place in the false self system, the lack of a parallel mechanism for identifying and letting go of "pleasurable emotions" caused by the *appeasement* of false self programs keeps the Divine Therapy heavily tied to relief of symptoms rather than the genuine impartial seeing necessary for ego-transcendence. Further refinement of the "Welcoming Practice" by David Frenette and others has begun to identify and correct that mistake; see ahead, Chapter 13.
3. Both this teaching and the "archeological dig," mentioned shortly below, are most fully developed in Keating's chapter "The Psychology of Centering Prayer" in *Intimacy with God* (New York: Crossroad, 1994), pp. 72–91.
4. Or *dissolve* into the true self, for that matter. As long as we are in the body, egoic functioning remains as a discrete operating system, necessary not only to maintain well-being but also to manifest true self within the limitations of this world. According to many schools of inner work, it's not so much a question of dismantling the egoic self as

of an intelligent interweaving of higher (Divine Indwelling or Spirit), lower (created essence, reflected through ego), and reconciling third (magnetic center, or heart) that brings about the conditions for the manifestation of true self. Take away any one of these and the manifestation collapses. The "New Man" that St. Paul refers to as the final goal of transformation is not the human being devoid of all personal characteristics, but one in whom the characteristics have become balanced and radiant through the work of this deeper integration. We will be looking more thoroughly at the development of magnetic center, or heart, in Chapters 11 and 12.

5. For a further development of this point, see my article "Nurturing the Heart" in *Parabola* 27, no. 1 (Spring 2002): 6–11.

6. Jansenism was a seventeenth-century heresy, particularly prevalent in Irish and French Catholicism, that saw the body as ontologically corrupt and itself an impediment to salvation.

7. Michael Washburn, *The Ego and the Dynamic Ground* (Albany, NY: State University of New York Press, 1988). Washburn's work was one of the principal formative influences as Keating developed his model of the divine therapy.

8. Thomas Keating reports that although there has been a vigorous recent attempt among the leadership of Contemplative Outreach to refer to groups simply as "Centering Prayer groups," fondness for the old terminology of "support group" remains strong at the grassroots level.

### Chapter 11: Attention of the Heart

1. John Main, *Word into Silence* (London: Darton, Longman and Todd, 1980). Republished in a collected edition as *The Inner Christ* (Darton, Longman and Todd, 1987), p. 68.

2. Private correspondence with Mary Jo Meadow, a well-known teacher of Christian Vipassana and other traditional meditation methods, April 20, 1999.

3. Some of the most illuminating research under way today is in the field of neuromeditation, where meditators are wired up to brainwave machines and their brainwave patterns monitored and compared. According to Dr. Marshall Voris, one of the pioneers in this field, the various meditation disciplines have characteristic and strikingly different brainwave signatures. Centering Prayer works characteristically in the alpha band, he reports (8–10 hertz), with striking plunges into theta (6–8 hertz), evidently during times of the unloading of the unconscious. (Unpublished research shared in a private conversation June 8, 2003)

4. This essay is found in *Writings from the Philokalia*, pp. 152–61. (See endnote 2, above.)

5. *Ibid.*, p. 158. Simeon's literal words here are: "In a word, he who does not have attention in himself . . . cannot become pure in heart and so cannot see God. He who does not have attention in himself cannot be poor in spirit, cannot weep and be contrite, nor be gentle and meek, nor hunger and thirst after righteousness, nor be merciful, nor a peacemaker, nor suffer persecution for righteousness' sake."

6. *Ibid.*, p. 153.
7. *Ibid.*
8. *Ibid.*, p. 154
9. Jacob Needleman, *Lost Christianity* (New York: Doubleday, 1980), p. 211.
10. *Writings from the Philokalia*, p. 154.
11. *Ibid.*, p. 158.
12. Philip Booth, "Heading Out," from *Lifelines* (New York: Viking Press, 1999), p. 199.
13. Thomas Merton, *The Hidden Ground of Love*, ed. William H. Shannon (New York: Farrar, Straus and Giroux, 1985), p. 64.
14. Sara Sviri, *The Taste of Hidden Things* (Inverness, CA: The Golden Sufi Center, 1997), pp. 135–36.
15. If you are comfortable with the language of chakras, in Centering Prayer you are working directly with the third chakra, the seat of the will.
16. Thomas Merton, "True Freedom," transcribed from the cassette series *Sufism: Longing for God* (Kansas City: Credence Cassettes, 1995). Merton is not specifically talking about magnetic center in the more technical way that I've just described it, but his understanding of what this inner center is and how it works is completely compatible.

### Chapter 12: Working with an Inner Observer
1. Eckhart Tolle, *The Power of Now: A Guide to Spiritual Enlightenment* (Vancouver, BC: Namaste Publishing, Inc., 1997), p. 152.
2. *Ibid.*, pp. 62–63.
3. René Daumal, *Mount Analogue* (Boston: Shambhala, 1986), p. 88.

### Chapter 13: The Welcoming Prayer
1. For information, contact the office of Contemplative Outreach, which publishes a regular newsletter listing retreats and training workshops available nationally and internationally. Full contact information is included at the end of this book.
2. The most current thinking within the Contemplative Outreach training workshops prefers not to designate a specific emotion or physical pain, but simply to use the word "Welcome": "as the symbol of your intention and consent to the presence and action of the indwelling Spirit in and through the distressing feeling or physical pain," as the guidelines now read. My own preference is to articulate the ballpark emotion or physical distress because, as we'll see shortly, the mind will tend automatically to fill in an object, and having a completely wrong object in one's head can lead to the misperception that the welcoming is a blanket condoning of situations that are in fact intolerable and require remediative action. Being able to name a ballpark object aids immeasurably in strengthening one's skill at inner observation. But the point is well taken that this articulation needs to remain general and simple; if it turns into minute self-analysis, the power of the prayer is undercut.
3. Ursula Le Guin, *A Wizard of Earthsea* (New York: Bantam Books, 1989).
4. Gerald May, *Will and Spirit: A Contemplative Psychology* (San Francisco: Harper and Row, 1982), pp. 197–99.

5. Maurice Nicoll, *Psychological Commentaries on the Teachings of Gurdjieff and Ouspensky*, vol. 5 (Boulder, CO: Shambhala, 1984), p. 543.
6. Jacob Boehme, *The Way to Christ*, trans. Peter Erb (Mahwah, NJ: Paulist Press, 1978), p. 240.

## Chapter 14: Centering Prayer and Christian Life
1. Thomas Merton, *The Seven Storey Mountain* (New York: Harcourt, Brace and World, 1948).
2. Thomas Merton, "A Member of the Human Race," quoted from Thomas P. McDonnell, ed., *A Thomas Merton Reader* (New York: Doubleday, 1989), p. 346.
3. "Binding Head and Heart," a conference convened by Fr. Thomas Keating and the Rev. David Keller with support from The Trust for Meditation Process, Minneapolis, MN; October 2–6, 2003, at St. Benedict's Monastery, Snowmass, CO. Participants in this initial exploratory conference were Jeannette A. Bakke, Cynthia Bourgeault, Tilden Edwards, Thomas G. Hand, Glenn Hinson, Thomas Keating, David Keller, Patrick J. Mitchell, Richard Rohr, Helen Rolfson, Nancy Roth, and Mary White. Quoted with permission.
4. This insight came to me via the Rev. Marianne Borg (Marcus's wife), during a conference in Portland, Oregon, January 21–22, 2001.

## Epilogue: The Way of the Heart
1. Kabir Helminski, *Living Presence: A Sufi Way to Mindfulness and the Essential Self* (New York: Tarcher/Putnam, 1992), p. 157.

# Books and Resources on Centering Prayer

**Books by Thomas Keating:**
*Awakenings*. New York: Crossroad, 1990.
*The Better Part: Stages of Contemplative Living*. New York: Continuum, 2000.
*Foundations for Centering Prayer and the Christian Contemplative Life*. New York: Continuum, 2002. (Combines *Open Mind, Open Heart*; *Invitation to Love*; and *The Mystery of the Liturgy* in a single volume.)
*Fruits and Gifts of the Spirit*. New York: Lantern Books, 2000.
*The Human Condition*. Mahwah, NJ: Paulist Press, 1999.
*Intimacy with God*. New York: Crossroad, 1994.
*Invitation to Love*. Rockport, MA: Element Books, 1992.
*The Kingdom of God is Like. . . .* New York: Crossroad, 1993.
*The Mystery of Christ*. Rockport, MA: Element Books, 1987.
*Open Mind, Open Heart*. Rockport, MA: Element Books, 1986.
*Reawakenings*. New York: Crossroad, 1993.

**Books by M. Basil Penington**
*Centering Prayer: Renewing an Ancient Christian Prayer Form*. New York: Image Books, 1982.
*Lectio Divina: Renewing an Ancient Practice of Praying the Scriptures*. New York: Crossroad, 1998.

**Books by Cynthia Bourgeault**
*Mystical Hope*. Cambridge, MA: Cowley Publications, 2001.
"Nurturing the Heart," *Parabola*, Vol. 27, No. 1 (spring 2002), pp. 6-10.
*The Wisdom Way of Knowing: Reclaiming an Ancient Tradition to Awaken the Heart*. San Francisco: Jossey-Bass, 2003.

For a listing of Centering Prayer retreats and support groups internationally, and general information, catalogs, and newsletters, contact:
Contemplative Outreach
P.O. Box 737
10 Park Place, Suite 2B
Butler, NJ 07405
Tel: 973-838-3384
Fax: 973-492-5795
Email: office@coutreach.org
Website: www.contemplativeoutreach.org

For a complete listing of books, audiotapes, and videotapes available through Contemplative Outreach, contact:
The Contemplative Outreach Media Center
375 Stewart Road, P.O. Box 1211
Wilkes-Barre, PA 18773-1211.
Phone 1-800-608-0096
Fax Order Form: 1-570-822-8226